6-13

A Friday the 13th Movie Trivia Book

Gene DeRosa

6-13 A Friday the 13th Movie Trivia Book

www.samsonpublishingcompany.com

Samson Publishing Company LLC

ISBN-13: 978-0692242346
ISBN-10: 0692242341

FIRST EDITION

DEDICATION

To my Editor, also known as my amazing wife, Traci, who has supported me in all ways for fifteen years now and has allowed me to "follow my dreams," regardless of how crazy they may seem.

CONTENTS

FOREWORD

In the summer of 1979, a group of filmmakers and actors led by Sean S. Cunningham gathered at Camp No-Be-Bo-Sco in Blairstown, New Jersey to make a horror film. It was a sunny, hot summer, during an era that witnessed a lot of major changes for the USA. "My Sharona" by The Knack and "Y.M.C.A." by The Village People were blasting out of car radios everywhere and the horrific *Sweeney Todd* and *The Elephant Man* were given Tony Awards. Sid Vicious was on trial for killing his girlfriend and it looked like the end for the mainstream popularity of punk rock. I was living in Westport, Connecticut then, and I had been in one feature film already – *Manny's Orphans*, also directed by Mr. Cunningham. I remember getting a phone call from Sean, who asked the famous question, "Can you swim?" I was cast as the Young Jason Voorhees over the phone in that moment. The production company that made *Friday the 13th* was based in Westport, and I had originally auditioned for the team at the Westport Y.M.C.A.

Working with special effects master Tom Savini was a young actor's dream become real. It took several weeks to create the molds for the mask, and I got to work at Tom's FX studio, which was like being invited into Merlin's workshop or a mad scientist's laboratory. Everywhere I looked, there were decapitated heads, severed limbs, weaponry of all types, explosives devices – everything that you could imagine for the creation of authentic and accurate special effects. Tom and his assistant, Taso Stavrakis, were a lot of fun to be around, and this energy carried over to the set when we arrived there in New Jersey. The entire cast and crew were hired from the NYC theatrical scene, so everyone was grateful to get out of the brutally hot summer in the city and spend some time making a fun film by Crystal Lake, which is actually known as Sand Pond. We all lived in the same cabins that are in the film, and ate our meals in the same kitchen area that they show in the film. It was a great deal of fun to be a 14-year-old actor on the set of *Friday the 13th*.

I was already studying jazz piano seriously at the time the film was made. One of the things I remember best about being on the set was how many of the crewmembers took an active interest in my musicianship. Very often, they would come around and bring me cassettes or even 8-track tapes (remember those?) to listen to of their favorite bands. Braden Lutz, who was in charge of the lighting, recommended Patti Smith and The Sex Pistols; others played The Ramones, The Damned, and Bad Brains. Barry Abrams, the director of photography and a wily Texan, always told me I looked like the famous comedian Kinky Friedman – another famous Texan, and he played his tapes for me. Back then, it was common to listen to tapes of Richard Pryor, Steve Martin, and other comedians. There was also a comedian right there with us on the set who would help us pass the time by telling jokes. Irwin Keyes, who played the busboy, but is for some reason uncredited (good trivia question), is a hilarious story-teller and comic. He would always tell us jokes to pass the time, but of course when I was there he would censor some of the raw parts, because I was only 14. The cast and crew worked well together and had fun, and I feel this empowered their productivity as a team.

When it was time to put on the makeup, I would have to get up around 3 AM to make a 4 AM set call. It took four hours to apply the entire makeup, but Tom and Taso made it easy and even enjoyable. The main focus was creating the right mood that allowed me to be able to get into character. We were all aware that there was such a brief moment of screen time that the entire scare would be based on how I looked for only a matter of seconds! I remember thinking that if I had no lines, then okay, I will convey the character's pain and desire for revenge through his eyes. Then I was told that one eye would be a glass eye! Therefore, I resolved to show it all through one eye and Jason's body language. In my mind, Jason came back to life when his mother's blood touched the water of Crystal Lake, and he instantly sought revenge for her death. To get into character, I would walk around the lake and look deeply into its waters, thinking about what it would mean to be a lake zombie child. Kevin Bacon even asked me what I was doing when he saw me, and I told him "I am getting into character," very seriously. He laughed very hard at that, called Harry Crosby over, and asked me the question again; I said, "I am getting into character. Don't you guys do that?" At this, they both laughed even harder and Kevin said "No, we are just trying to get into the female characters hahaha..." I got the joke finally; here was a little kid all serious about playing Jason Voorhees!

Now I have a band called FIRST JASON and we tour all over the US and Europe, having performed an almost every state, as well as Spain, Italy, France, Germany, Holland, and the UK. We have two albums out. The first is "JASON IS WATCHING!" and the new release is "HEED MY WARNING." There are videos on YouTube for "Jason's Bride" and "Victim," as well as "First Jason Live at Viper Room." It is an absolute thrill to rock out with audiences that share a love of *Friday the 13th* and Jason Voorhees. One of the fun things we always do is ask trivia questions to the audience like "What was Jason's mother's name?" and "Who composed the soundtrack to *Friday the 13th*?" We give out prizes to those who know the correct answers. Camp Crystal Lake is indeed a treasure trove of trivia. There are so many films and so many great actors, special effects masters, directors, and composers to identify, plus amazing locations to re-discover. *6 - 13 A Friday the 13th Movie Trivia Book* is the perfect accompaniment to a night of *Friday the 13th* fun with friends at home or at a local pub. I welcome everyone to return to Camp Crystal Lake where Mama Voorhees is waiting for you, and remember . . .

JASON NEVER DIES!!! Ari Lehman/FIRST JASON

ACKNOWLEDGMENTS

Thanks to:

Sean S. Cunningham, Victor Miller, Ron Kurz, and Tom Savini for creating the *Friday the 13th* movie franchise and everybody's favorite slasher, Jason Voorhees. Thank you for getting an almost-10-year-old little boy hooked on horror (after he overcame his initial terror)!

My childhood friends Craig and Lenny, who will probably never see this, but still deserve some credit for helping my admiration for horror movies grow.

All my trivia friends, some of which have been around even longer than my wife, for feeding my addiction for all sorts of knowledge – even the stuff no one other than me knows or cares about.

All the Facebook fans! Things were looking a bit bleak before you came along. I certainly hope the book can live up to your expectations.

David Spillers for purchasing my first book sold to someone I didn't know! It is a huge step! Thanks to Alan Clague for letting me use one of his questions in the book.

James Maxwell, who actually chose the IndieGoGo reward to get a thank you and a copy of the book, and who contributed a question for the book. Honestly though, he probably would have gotten his name here for being the most active and enthusiastic of those Facebook fans. Thanks, James!

Richard Gray Pennington of Elite Stone Replicas, aka the Maker of the Masks. Thanks for jumping on board and helping out with the project. I am sure this will grow into a prosperous endeavor and friendship.

Diogo Landô, who did the incredible cover art for the book. Thanks, Diogo, for a job well done, being very easy to work with, and for knowing not to pay much attention to that first rambling e-mail response I would always send after seeing each step of the process taking form. Most importantly, thanks for taking my vision and making it happen in an amazing way.

Ari Lehman for being a great guy and even talking to some weird stranger who sent him a Facebook message proposing crazy ideas. Thanks for helping out with the IndieGoGo rewards, the use of the music, and for being open to ideas. Thanks most for after talking to me for a brief time, expressing how you felt about the book idea, and for without hesitation agreeing to write the foreword for the book when I asked. Thanks, Ari; Jason Never Dies, especially The First Jason!

Finally, just because the book is dedicated to her doesn't mean she doesn't get a huge thank you! Thank you to my amazing wife, Traci! Thank you for all the support, all the help, all the taking of gibberish and forming it into complete thoughts that all will understand, all the eyerolls for the really out-there ideas, and just for being you, and loving me.

QUESTIONS

"We ain't gonna stand for no weirdness out here."
– Officer Dorf (Friday the 13th (1980))

AM I EVIL?

Answers on page 131

1) When was Jason Voorhees born?
2) Who is Jason's mother?
3) Who is Jason's father?
4) What was the name of Jason's sister?
5) In what cemetery was Jason's body once buried?
6) In what year did Jason drown in Crystal Lake?
7) In what year did authorities begin trying to execute Jason by means of electrocution, gas, firing squad, and even hanging?
8) What medical condition does Jason suffer from, the results of which explain his appearance in the original *Friday the 13th*?

6-13

KILLER MOMMY

Answers on page 132

1) In what year was Pamela Voorhees born?
   a. 1930
   b. 1933
   c. 1936
   d. 1939

2) In what year was Pamela Voorhees killed by Alice Hardy in the original *Friday the* 13th?
   a. 1977
   b. 1979
   c. 1981
   d. 1983

3) How many different people have portrayed some part of Mrs. Pamela Voorhees in the *Friday the* 13th films?
   a. 3
   b. 4
   c. 5
   d. 6

4) What was Pamela Voorhees's position at Camp Crystal Lake at the time of Jason's drowning?
   a. Maid
   b. Cook
   c. Archery instructor
   d. Head counselor

5) What article of clothing was included in Jason's shrine to his mother, along with her head, in the *Friday the* 13th *Part 2*?
   a. Sweater
   b. Hat
   c. Shoes
   d. Scarf

6) According to the opening of the 2009 *Friday the* 13th reboot, in what year was Mrs. Voorhees decapitated?
   a. 1978
   b. 1979
   c. 1980
   d. 1981

CAMP CRYSTAL LAKE

Answers on page 133

1) In what year was Camp Crystal Lake created?

2) What family created Camp Crystal Lake?

3) What is the nickname given to Camp Crystal Lake after the 1958 murders?

4) In what state is Camp Crystal Lake located?

5) Who is the owner and boss at Camp Crystal Lake in Part 1?

6) What fictitious county is listed on the ambulance that takes Jason's body away at the beginning of *Friday the 13th: The Final Chapter* (Part 4)?

7) What did they change the name of Crystal Lake to in *Jason Lives: Friday the 13th Part VI*?

8) What is the name of the county where Crystal Lake is located *in Jason Goes to Hell: The Final Friday* (Part 9)?

9) What was the name of the Boy Scout camp that was used as Camp Crystal Lake in the original *Friday the 13th* (1980)?

#SLASHTAGS

Answers on page 134

Match these taglines with their movies:

1) Camp Crystal Lake's bloody legacy!
2) Evil always rises again.
3) Even a killer has something to fear.
4) On Friday the 13th, Jason is back. But this time, someone's waiting.
5) They were warned…They are doomed…And on Friday the 13th, nothing will save them.
6) Evil gets an upgrade.
7) Jason lives. Many will die.
8) Jason's back, and this is the one you've been screaming for.
9) Just when you thought it was safe to go back to camp.
10) The mindless, murderous fury that was buried with Jason has been reborn. And suddenly, terror has become child's play!
11) Evil has finally found a home.
12) The city that has seen it all ain't seen nothing yet!

#SLASHTAGS

a. *Friday the 13th (1980)*

b. *Friday the 13th Part 2*

c. *Friday the 13th Part 3*

d. *Friday the 13th: The Final Chapter*

e. *Friday the 13th: A New Beginning*

f. *Jason Lives: Friday the 13th Part VI*

g. *Friday the 13th Part VII: The New Blood*

h. *Friday the 13th Part VIII: Jason Takes Manhattan*

i. *Jason Goes to Hell: The Final Friday*

j. *Jason X*

k. *Freddy vs. Jason*

l. *Friday the 13th (2009)*

CAMP COUNSELORS

Answers on page 135

1) Which counselor was going to be the cook, but never made it to Camp Crystal Lake in the original *Friday the 13th*?
2) Which counselor found a snake in their cabin in *Friday the 13th*?
3) Which counselor is confined to a wheelchair in *Friday the 13th Part 2*?
4) What caused him to become paralyzed and confined to the wheelchair?
5) Who is in charge of the Packanack Lake Region Counselor Training Center, which is where most of the action occurs in *Friday the 13th Part 2*?
6) Whose dead body was lying next to Jason the first time we see him face to face (or is that face to sack?) in *Friday the 13th Part 2*?
7) Who were the head counselors at Camp Forest Green, who never actually make it to camp, in *Jason Lives: Friday the 13th Part VI*?
8) Which counselor had her head torn off in *Jason Lives: Friday the 13th Part VI*?

"Being dead wasn't a problem, but being forgotten, now that's a bitch."
– Freddy Krueger (Freddy vs. Jason)

THE MEN BEHIND THE MASK

Answers on page 136

1) True or false: Jason Voorhees was once portrayed by a woman.
2) Who is the only actor, other than Kane Hodder, to portray Jason in more than one *Friday the 13th* film, not counting flashback archive footage?
3) Which actor was the first one to wear the hockey mask while portraying Jason?
4) Which actor had a stunt go horribly wrong early in his career, which left him with third-degree burns over 50% of his body?
5) Despite Warrington Gillette being credited as Jason in Part 2, what stuntman portrayed him for all but the final scene?
6) Which *Friday the 13th* movie has the most actors shown as Jason in both flashback archive footage and the current film's action?
7) Which Jason actor demanded at the end of shooting that his name be removed from the film?
8) At 6 foot-5 inches tall, who was the tallest actor to have played Jason?

WHO ARE YOU?

This is a comprehensive list of every person that has portrayed some part of Jason Voorhees in the *Friday the 13th* films.

Actor	Film	Notes
Ari Lehman	*Friday the 13th*	The First Jason
Ellen Lutter	*Friday the 13th Part 2*	Costume designer who portrayed Jason's legs as he approaches Alice's house
Warrington Gillette	*Friday the 13th Part 2*	Was only Jason in the final scene
Steve Daskawicz *known as Steve Dash*	*Friday the 13th Part 2*	Uncredited stuntman who was Jason throughout most of the film
Richard Brooker	*Friday the 13th Part 3*	First to wear the mask
Ted White	*Friday the 13th: The Final Chapter*	Demanded his name be removed from credits
Tom Morga	*Friday the 13th: A New Beginning*	Portrayed Jason in the dream sequences and the imposter Jason in the blue mask
Dan Bradley	*Jason Lives: Friday the 13th Part VI*	Did one day of shooting: the paintball scenes
C.J. Graham	*Jason Lives: Friday the 13th Part VI*	Stuntman; studio thought Bradley was too bulky

Actor	Film	Notes
Kane Hodder	*Part VII: the New Blood, Part VIII: Jason Takes Manhattan, Jason Goes to Hell, Jason X*	Portrayed Jason in 4 films; considered the best Jason by many
Tim Mirkovich	*Friday the 13th Part VIII: Jason Takes Manhattan*	Young Jason
Ken Kirzinger	*Friday the 13th Part VIII: Jason Takes Manhattan, Freddy vs. Jason*	Stand-in for Kane Hodder in some scenes as Jason
Spencer Stump	*Freddy vs. Jason*	Young Jason
Douglas Tait	*Freddy vs. Jason*	Was Jason in some scenes that needed to be reshot when Kirzinger was not available, including the final shot where Jason emerges from Camp Crystal Lake carrying Freddy's head
Derek Mears	*Friday the 13th (2009)*	
Caleb Guss	*Friday the 13th (2009)*	Young Jason

6-13

MOMMY DEAREST

These women played Jason's mother . . . or at least parts of her.

Actress	**Film**	**Notes**
Betsy Palmer	*Friday the 13th*	The original Mrs. Pamela Voorhees
Connie Hogan	*Friday the 13th Part 2*	The head on the shrine
Marilyn Poucher	*Friday the 13th Part 3*	The corpse that leaps from the water
Paula Shaw	*Freddy vs. Jason*	Used as Freddy's pawn to manipulate Jason
Nana Visitor	*Friday the 13th (2009)*	Briefly appears at the start before she is beheaded

JASONS' RESUMES

Answers on page 137

1) Which Jason actor has appeared in four *Star Trek* TV series (*The Next Generation, Voyager, Deep Space Nine, Enterprise*), as well as *Star Trek: The Motion Picture* and *Star Trek VI: The Undiscovered Country*?
2) Which Jason actor's only other acting credit was as "Sgt. Bedlam, Hellcop" alongside Gilbert Gottfried's portrayal of Hitler in *Highway to Hell* (1991)?
3) Which Jason actor portrayed various characters in the 1965-70 TV series *Daniel Boone*?
4) Which Jason actor was honored with an "In Memory Of" tag at the end of an episode of Gordon Ramsay's *Hell's Kitchen* upon his death in 2013?
5) Which Jason actor portrayed Dennis Rader (the B.T.K. Killer), as well as murderer and body-snatcher Ed Gein, who inspired the creation of characters like Norman Bates of *Psycho* and Leatherface of *The Texas Chainsaw Massacre*?
6) Which Jason actor portrayed one of Abed and Troy's favorite movie characters, Kickpuncher, on the TV series *Community*?
7) Which Jason actor had previously appeared in a *Friday the 13th* movie as a victim of Jason?

6-13

"You're doomed! You're all doomed!"
– Crazy Ralph (Friday the 13th (1980))

TOWNSFOLK

Answers on page 138

1) What was the name of the man that gives Annie a ride from the Country Grocer in town out to The Crossroads halfway to Camp Crystal Lake in the original *Friday the 13th*?
2) What is the name of the town "crazy" who warns he is a messenger of God in the first two films?
3) What was the name of the motorcycle gang that Shelly and Vera have a run-in with at the store in *Friday the 13th Part 3*?
4) What is the name of the old man who owns the land Donnie works on and the tow truck in the 2009 *Friday the 13th* reboot?
5) What is the name of the crazy, ultra-redneck woman that lives next to Pinehurst Youth Development Center in *Friday the 13th: A New Beginning*?
6) What is the name of the caretaker at the Eternal Peace Cemetery where Jason was buried in *Jason Lives: Friday the 13th Part VI*?
7) In *Jason Lives: Friday the 13th Part VI*, Larry, Stan, Katie, Burt, and Roy are seen at a corporate retreat participating in what activity?

GRIM FACTS

Answers on page 139

1) What is the name of the company that Enos drives a truck for in the original *Friday the 13th*?
   a. Hazzard Oil Supply
   b. Stanhope Waste Co.
   c. Elston Oil Supply
   d. Franklin Township Water
2) Where did Ginny discover Crazy Ralph's dead body in *Friday the 13th Part 2*?
   a. The pantry
   b. In a canoe on the lake
   c. The shower
   d. Her bed
3) What were the names of the couple who ran the Crystal Lake Variety Store seen at the beginning of *Friday the 13th Part 3*?
   a. Harold and Maude
   b. Stan and Bea
   c. Garret and Beverly
   d. Harold and Edna
4) What was the name of the old man sleeping in the middle of the road that the van almost runs over, who then tells the group they are all doomed in Part 3?
   a. Abel
   b. Job
   c. Cain
   d. Noah

5) What were the names of the three members of The Black Widows motorcycle gang seen in *Friday the 13th Part 3*?
   a. Frank, Missy, and Mark
   b. Ali, Fox, and Loco
   c. Will, Sally, and Mongoose
   d. Ronnie, Bobbie, and Ricky

6) What is the name of the coroner who is the first person to be killed in *Friday the 13th: The Final Chapter*?
   a. Duff
   b. Axel
   c. Steven
   d. Slash

7) What is the name of the waitress that Billy is waiting for when he is killed in *Friday the 13th: A New Beginning*?
   a. Lana
   b. Chloe
   c. Lois
   d. Martha

8) What were the names of the two kids in the car dressed more like they should have been in *The Outsiders* than a *Friday the 13th* movie in Part 5?
   a. Vinny and Bobby
   b. Jimmy and Clark
   c. Ash and Sam
   d. Pete and Vinnie

LOCATION, LOCATION, LOCATION

Each film took place in a distinct location in and around Crystal Lake (with a couple of exceptions). Here is where the bulk of the action took place in each film.

Film	Location
Friday the 13th	Camp Crystal Lake
Friday the 13th Part 2	Packanack Lake Region Counselor Training Center
Friday the 13th Part 3	Higgins Haven
Friday the 13th: The Final Chapter	The Jarvis house and neighboring house, a moderate distance from Crystal Point
Friday the 13th: A New Beginning	Pinehurst Youth Development Center
Jason Lives: Friday the 13th Part VI	Forest Green / Camp Forest Green
Friday the 13th Part VII: The New Blood	The Shepard house and neighboring house
Friday the 13th Part VIII: Jason Takes Manhattan	Aboard the SS *Lazarus* and Manhattan
Jason Goes to Hell: The Final Friday	Crystal Lake (more of a town area setting)
Jason X	Crystal Lake Research Facility / The *Grendel*
Freddy vs. Jason	Springwood, Ohio / Camp Crystal Lake
Friday the 13th (2009)	Camp Crystal Lake

"This sucks on so many levels."
– Janessa (Jason X)

ON LOCATION

While the films had their roots in New Jersey, they moved around quite a bit over time. Here are the actual filming locales.

Film	Filming Locales	Notes
Friday the 13th	Blairstown, NJ Hope, NJ Freehold, NJ	Camp No-Be-Bo-Sco is in Blairstown. Hope can be seen during Enos and Annie's drive. The final hospital scene is in Freehold.
Friday the 13th Part 2	Kent, CT New Preston, CT	KenWood Camp is in Kent. The bar scene was shot in New Preston, CT.
Friday the 13th Part 3	Newhall, CA Santa Clarita, CA	Shelly and Vera's store scene was filmed at Spunky Canyon Market in the Green Valley in Newhall. They covered the walls with New Jersey-related items like a Pick-It lottery sign and an ad for a flea market on Route 206 in Newton, NJ. The rest was purpose-built sets on a studio lot in Santa Clarita.

Film	Filming Locales	Notes
Friday the 13th: The Final Chapter	Topanga Canyon in Los Angeles, CA Santa Clarita, CA	The opening scenes were done at the same Melody Ranch set in Santa Clarita. The Jarvis house and surrounding areas were off of N. Topanga Canyon Boulevard in L.A.
Friday the 13th: A New Beginning	Camarillo, CA	Camarillo is conveniently located off the Ventura Freeway (The 101) between Thousand Oaks and Ventura, CA.
Jason Lives: Friday the 13th Part VI	Rutledge, GA	Hard Labor Creek State Park in Rutledge, about 50 miles east of Atlanta, was used.
Friday the 13th Part VII: The New Blood	Mobile, Alabama Los Angeles, CA	Mobile and surrounding areas. An Alabama license plate on the Shepards' car is visible as they arrive at their Crystal Lake house. Robin's death scene where she is thrown out the window was actually filmed at the Jarvis house from *The Final Chapter* because it had to be reshot.

Film	Filming Locales	Notes
Friday the 13th Part VIII: Jason Takes Manhattan	Vancouver, British Columbia, Canada Los Angeles, CA Manhattan, NYC	Most of the film was shot in Vancouver. The rest was shot in Manhattan. However, in an odd moneysaving move, the alleyway and wharf scenes were shot in L.A.
Jason Goes to Hell: The Final Friday	Los Angeles, CA	This explains why it is more of an in-town setting with so few "Crystal Lake"-looking locales.
Jason X	Toronto, Ontario, Canada	Space can be filmed just about anywhere.
Freddy vs. Jason	Vancouver, British Columbia, Canada	It was the first time a Freddy movie had been shot outside the U.S., and they had to do an extensive search to find a house that looked similar enough to the original 1428 Elm Street house.
Friday the 13th (2009)	Austin, TX	Filmed entirely in and around the Austin area.

"I've seen enough horror movies to know any weirdo wearing a mask is never friendly."
– Lizabeth Mott (Jason Lives: Friday the 13th Part VI)

IT FEELS LIKE THE FIRST TIME

Answers on page 140

1) Which was the first *Friday the 13th* movie not to be a #1 movie for a weekend, and also not to break $20 million at the box office?
2) What was the first *Friday the 13th* film to actually premiere in theaters on Friday the 13th?
3) The first time that Jason strangled someone with his bare hands was a girl named Eva in which movie?
4) Kyle Labine, who portrayed Bill Freeburg in *Freddy vs. Jason*, became the first person to appear in a movie with Freddy, Jason, and Michael Myers as he had previously been in which *Halloween* movie?
5) In which film did Jason first get shot?
6) What weapon was used to kill Jason the first time we see him left for dead at the end of a *Friday the 13th* movie?
7) Not counting all the flashback dream scenes, who is the only person Freddy Krueger actually kills in *Freddy vs. Jason*?

I SLASHED THE SHERIFF

Answers on page 141

Match the law enforcement officer to the proper question.

1) What was the name of the motorcycle officer that comes to Camp Crystal Lake looking for Crazy Ralph in the original *Friday the 13th*?
2) What is the name of the first member of law enforcement to be killed by Jason?
3) Which member of law enforcement tried to help stop Freddy and Jason in *Freddy vs. Jason* but wound up dead?
4) Which law enforcement officer was part of one of the most memorable kills when Jason grabs him and bends him backwards in half to the point that his feet are behind his shoulders?
5) Which member of law enforcement had recently broken up with Diana Kimble (Jason's sister) in *Jason Goes to Hell: The Final Friday*?
6) Which member of law enforcement killed no one, despite the fact that Jason had taken over his body in *Jason Goes to Hell: The Final Friday*?

a. Sheriff Ed Landis
b. Deputy Scott Stubbs
c. Officer Dorf
d. Sheriff Michael Garris
e. Officer Randy Parker
f. Deputy Winslow

THIS TIME (WILL BE THE LAST TIME)

Answers on page 142

1) In what year do the events depicted in the original *Friday the 13th* take place?
2) In what year do the events seen in *Friday the 13th Part 2, Friday the 13th Part 3, and Friday the 13th: The Final Chapter* all take place?
3) In what year do the scenes in space take place in *Jason X*?

Which of these events took place first in the original timeline (excluding the 2009 reboot)?

A. Jason was shot for the first time OR
B. Jason strangled someone with his bare hands

C. Richard Brooker portrayed Jason Voorhees OR
D. Ted White portrayed Jason Voorhees

E. Jason Voorhees is struck by lightning OR
F. Jason Voorhees electrocutes someone to death

G. Paul Holt runs a site near Crystal Lake OR
H. Matthew Letter runs a site near Crystal Lake

I. A dog named Gordon appeared in the movies OR
J. A dog named Toby appeared in the movies

K. We were introduced to the Eternal Peace Cemetery OR
L. We were introduced to Higgins Haven

6-13

WHAT A PAIR

Answers on page 143

1) What were the names of the two stoners in *Friday the 13th Part 3*?
2) What were the names of the twin girls in *Friday the 13th: The Final Chapter*?
3) What couple were speared together while having sex in *Friday the 13th Part 2* in a scene that had to be trimmed to avoid an X rating?
4) What is the name of Reggie's brother and his brother's girlfriend in *Friday the 13th: A New Beginning*?
5) Which two crewmembers of the *Grendel* sacrificed themselves in *Jason X*?
6) Which couple essentially breaks up when she takes a liking to Clay, and he sleeps with another woman in the *Friday the 13th* reboot?
7) Which couple was expecting a baby in *Friday the 13th Part 3*?

   a. Andy and Debbie

   b. Trent and Jenna

   c. Chuck and Chili

   d. Waylander and Brodski

   e. Tina and Terri

   f. Demon and Anita

   g. Jeff and Sandra

A WHOLE OTHER DIMENSION

Answers on page 144

1) Which food being cooked is used as one of the many tricks to take advantage of the 3-D effects of Part 3?
   a. Bacon
   b. Popcorn
   c. Cake
   d. Fried chicken

2) Which toy was used to take advantage of the 3-D effects of Part 3?
   a. Lawn darts
   b. Slip-N-Slide
   c. Paddle ball
   d. Yo-yo

3) What weapon was attached to a wire and shot so that the projectile would come straight at the camera in Part 3?
   a. Harpoon gun
   b. Knife
   c. Chinese throwing star
   d. Baseball bat

4) Whose head was squeezed until his eyeball flew out of his head to utilize the 3-D effect in Part 3?
   a. Shelly
   b. Ali
   c. Rick
   d. Andy

"Help! He's killing me! He's killing me!"
– Rob Dyer (Friday the 13th: The Final Chapter)

COOL KILLS

Answers on page 145

1) Who is the first person that Jason electrocutes to death?
2) Where was Demon when he was killed (by Roy) in *Friday the 13th: A New Beginning*?
3) What is the name of the female camper that is killed when Jason swings her, in her sleeping bag, into a tree?
4) What unusual murder weapon was used to kill Dr. Crews in *Friday the 13th Part VII: The New Blood*?
5) Whose head does Jason punch off in *Friday the 13th Part VIII: Jason Takes Manhattan*?
6) Who got sucked out through a small hole that Uber-Jason punched through the ship from the outside in *Jason X*?
7) Who can be seen spinning slowly down a large drill bit after being pushed over a railing and impaled on the bit in *Jason X*?
8) What does Jason thrust through Freddy's back, disabling him enough for Lori to decapitate him in *Freddy vs. Jason*?
9) Who had her head smashed into a mirror and into the side of the RV, leaving a detailed imprint of her face in *Jason Lives: Friday the 13th Part VI*?

10) In the 2009 reboot, we see Jason use a bow and arrow for the first time. He uses it to put an arrow through whose head while they are driving in a speed boat at a high rate of speed?

11) Crispin Glover's character Jimbo met his end with what unusual weapon being driven through his hand, followed by a cleaver to his head, in *Friday the 13th: The Final Chapter*?

12) Roy's first kill in *A New Beginning* was Vinnie, who had what emergency item shoved into his mouth?

13) Whose face is submerged in a sink full of liquid nitrogen and then smashed into a counter by Jason in *Jason X*?

14) Which character from *Friday the 13th Part VIII: Jason Takes Manhattan* got a much-deserved death by drowning?

15) In the 2009 *Friday the 13th* reboot, Jason drives his machete into Trent's chest and then shoves him backwards, where he is impaled on whose tow truck?

16) In *Friday the 13th Part VII: The New Blood*, Kate is killed by having what unusual murder weapon driven into her eye?

THE MASKS OF DEATH

Answers on page 146

1) What does Jason wear over his face in *Friday the 13th Part 2*?
2) Which character is first seen wearing the hockey mask that would eventually be made famous by Jason Voorhees?
3) The original mask used in *Friday the 13th Part 3* was a modified version of what National Hockey League team's goalie mask?
4) What is visually different about the hockey mask that Roy wears in *Friday the 13th: A New Beginning*?
5) When Jason climbs out of the water in Manhattan, what sports league is advertised on the billboard that he looks at?
6) Whose hockey mask does Jason take at the beginning of *Friday the 13th Part VIII: Jason Takes Manhattan*?
7) How does Jason get his mask back at the beginning of *Jason Lives: Friday the 13th Part VI*?
8) In which film did Jason actually lift his own mask to scare someone away?
9) Who had Jason just killed before finding his hockey mask in the 2009 *Friday the 13th* reboot?

WE ARE FAMILY

Throughout the movies, there have been quite a few familial relationships. Here is a list of them all.

Characters	Relationship	Notes
Sandra and Rob Dyer	Sister and brother	Sandra was in Part 2. Rob was in *Friday the 13th: The Final Chapter.*
Tina and Terri	Twin sisters	*Friday the 13th: The Final Chapter*
Trish and Tommy Jarvis and their unnamed mother	Sister, brother, and mother	The siblings were the only survivors of *Friday the 13th: The Final Chapter.*
Roy and Joey	Father and son	Paramedic Roy killed everyone while disguised as Jason after Joey was killed by Vic in *Friday the 13th: A New Beginning.*
Ethel and Junior Hubbard	Mother and son	Ultra-redneck family that lives next to Pinehurst in *Friday the 13th: A New Beginning.*
Reggie, Demon, and Gramps (George)	Brothers and their grandfather	Gramps is the cook at Pinehurst. Reggie, one of the survivors, is with him. Demon is visiting. All are in *Friday the 13th: A New Beginning.*

Characters	Relationship	Notes
Paula and Lizabeth Mott	Sisters	*Jason Lives: Friday the 13th Part VI*
Megan and Sheriff Michael Garris	Father and daughter	Sheriff Garris doesn't believe Tommy Jarvis's claims that Jason is alive, going as far as arresting him. His daughter Megan not only believes him, but helps him escape and fight Jason. All are in *Jason Lives: Friday the 13th Part VI.*
Nick and Michael	Cousins	The surprise party in *Friday the 13th Part VII: The New Blood* is for Michael. He never makes it to the party.
John, Amanda, and Tina Shepard	Father, mother, and daughter	Tina has telekinetic abilities. She kills her father early on, then becomes a formidable opponent for Jason in *Friday the 13th Part VII: The New Blood.*

Characters	Relationship	Notes
Rennie Wickham and Charles McCulloch	Niece and uncle/legal guardian	Rennie nearly drowned when her uncle pushed her into Camp Crystal Lake to teach her how to swim in *Friday the 13th Part VIII: Jason Takes Manhattan.*
Admiral Robertson and Sean Robertson	Father and son	The Admiral captained the SS *Lazarus*, and Sean was Rennie's boyfriend in *Friday the 13th Part VIII: Jason Takes Manhattan.*
Pamela, Elias, and Jason Voorhees; Diana Kimble, Jessica Kimble, and baby Stephanie	Mother, father, and son; daughter, granddaughter, and great-granddaughter	Pamela and Elias are Jason's parents. Diana Kimble is Jason's sister. Jessica is his niece, and Stephanie is her daughter. The last three are introduced in *Jason Goes to Hell: The Final Friday.* Diana is most likely Jason's half-sister as Pamela says Jason is an only child.

Characters	Relationship	Notes
Joey B, Shelby, and Ward	Mother, father, and son	The family ran the diner in *Jason Goes to Hell: The Final Friday.*
Dr. Campbell, his wife, and Lori Campbell	Father, mother, and daughter	Dr. Campbell killed his wife while possessed by Freddy. Lori was one of two survivors in *Freddy vs. Jason.*
Mark and Bobby Davis	Brothers	Freddy killed Bobby and made it look like suicide. Mark entered the psychiatric hospital soon after. Mark was then also killed by Freddy in *Freddy vs. Jason.*
Blake and Blake's Father	Father and son	Jason killed them both in *Freddy vs. Jason.*
Clay and Whitney Miller	Siblings	Survivors of *Friday the 13th* (2009)

"People go missing around here, they're gone for good. Outsiders come, they don't know where to walk. They bring trouble. We just want to be left alone. And so does he."
– Old Lady (Friday the 13th (2009))

DO IT AGAIN

Answers on page 147

All of these questions are about the 2009 franchise reboot.

1) Who does Jason chain up in his lair, rather than kill, at the end of the first day shown in the *Friday the 13th* reboot?
   a. Amanda
   b. Whitney
   c. Jenna
   d. Alice
2) What is the name of the gas station where Trent, Jenna, and the group stop and meet up with Clay for the first time?
   a. Outpost
   b. The Cube
   c. The Peach Pit
   d. The Palomino
3) What is the name of Chewie's bong?
   a. Betsy
   b. Ethel
   c. Lucille
   d. Jackie
4) Chewie, Lawrence, Trent, and Bree play what game in the *Friday the 13th* reboot?
   a. Beer Pong
   b. Angry Birds
   c. The Settlers of Catan
   d. Grand Theft Auto
5) Who gets caught in a bear trap near the edge of the campsite in the *Friday the 13th* reboot?
   a. Richie
   b. Ralph
   c. Clay
   d. Aaron

6) Trophies for what two sports can be seen in the cabin that Clay and Jenna go into near the beginning of their search of Camp Crystal Lake in the *Friday the 13th* reboot?
   a. Baseball and bowling
   b. Basketball and archery
   c. Archery and hockey
   d. Hockey and baseball

7) What item that Chewie finds in the tool shed does he suggests completes Jason's outfit in the *Friday the 13th* reboot?
   a. Necktie
   b. Pipe
   c. Hockey stick
   d. Potato sack

8) What does Lawrence use as a shield and a weapon when he goes out to check on Chewie in the tool shed?
   a. Wok and fire poker
   b. BBQ grill lid and tongs
   c. Frying pan and butcher knife
   d. Trash can lid and broomstick

9) What piece of machinery is used to help stop Jason in the *Friday the 13th* reboot?
   a. Generator
   b. Combine
   c. Wood chipper
   d. Reaper

10) What three snack foods does Chewie buy at the gas station?
   a. Doritos, Funyuns, and Twinkies
   b. Pretzels, donuts, and ice cream
   c. Combos, Fritos, and Funyuns
   d. Cheetos, Ruffles, and Combos

MACHETE IS MY FRIEND

There were many different means of death. Here they all are with the total number of kills each was used for. This is ALL kills, not just Jason's.

Weapon/Means	**Number of kills (original films)**	**Number of kills (reboot)**
Machete	32	7
Unseen and unknown	24	1 (Mike)
Long spikes, posts, or spears	13	
Head mutilated	11	
Axe	6	1
Cleaver	5	
Harpoons	5	
Butcher knife	4	
Electrocution	4	
Hull breach	4	
Hunting knife	4	
Impaled	3	
Neck snapped	3	
Possession	3	
Unknown knife	3	
Defenestration	2	
Drowned	2	
Fist	2	
Metal tent spike	2	
Pitchfork	2	
Fire poker, screwdriver, burned in sleeping bag, arrow, antlers		1 each

6-13

All of the following means were each used once in the original eleven films:

- arm broken/thrown into door
- axe handle
- bear hug
- bed of spikes
- bent in half backwards
- broken back
- broken whiskey bottle
- car explosion
- chain
- claw hammer
- drug needle
- elbow to face
- fire poker
- flare
- Freddy (face slash/burnt)
- fryer/grill
- hand rake
- grabbed and thrown
- guitar to head
- hacksaw
- head twisted off
- hedge trimming shears
- hot stones
- icepick
- knife sharpener
- knitting needle
- liquid nitrogen
- long handle grass hook
- Magic Dagger
- metal probe
- mirror glass shard
- party horn
- pole
- rifle stock
- shelf bracket
- shotgun blast
- sickle
- small metal spike
- smashed into tree
- strangled with bare hands
- sucked into space
- telekinesis
- thrown into mirror
- unknown weapon
- weed whacker with saw blade
- wire (garrote)
- wrench

Dream sequence and hologram kill methods not listed above: machete (5), bludgeoned (2), small metal spike (1)

SPACE ODDITY

Answers on page 148

1) What is the name of the realty company that is advertising "Lunar Estates" on an old billboard seen floating through space in *Jason X*?
2) What are the computerized medical regeneration particles called in *Jason X*?
3) What is the name of the ship that takes Rowan and Jason on board for further studies?
4) Where is the ship headed in *Jason X*?
5) According to *Jason X*, what sport was banned in 2024?
6) What is the name of the space station that the ship was going to dock with, but instead blows up, in *Jason X*?
7) What futuristic war was mentioned in *Jason X*?
8) Who crashes the escape shuttle into the main ship when they try to take off while the fuel line is still attached?
9) What is Jason referred to after he is regenerated by the ANTS and becomes partially metal?
10) How many holographic people does Jason kill in *Jason X*?
11) What was the specimen number given to Jason prior to him defrosting and going on a killing spree in space in *Jason X*?
    a. 613 b. 1313 c. 2455 d. 4420

CAMPFIRE SONGS

Answers on page 149

1) Fan-Submitted Question from Richard Gray Pennington: What Australian New Wave band provided the song "His Eyes" for *Friday the 13th: A New Beginning*?
2) What two songs are being sung by the counselors at the start of the original *Friday the 13th*?
3) What song does Doug sing while in the shower in *Friday the 13th: The Final Chapter*?
4) What song is playing while Cort is driving the RV in *Jason Lives: Friday the 13th Part VI*?
5) What were the call letters for the Manhattan radio station broadcasting all the way to Camp Crystal Lake at the beginning of *Friday the 13th Part VIII: Jason Takes Manhattan*?
6) What song is Wade listening to shortly before he is killed in the *Friday the 13th* reboot?
7) What rock song was actually being played during Crispin Glover's awkward dance scene and later had "Love Is a Lie" by Lion dubbed over it in *Friday the 13th: The Final Chapter*?
8) What musical artist's song titles were used as working titles for the *Friday the 13th* films to help prevent script leaks?

PSEUDOHYMNS

All but one of these were David Bowie song titles.

Film	Title Used for the Script	Notes
Friday the 13th Part 3	"Crystal Japan"	An instrumental Bowie released in 1980 in Japan as a single. The B-Side was "Alabama Song" which was made popular by The Doors
Friday the 13th: A New Beginning	"Repetition"	The 9th track on Bowie's 1979 album "Lodger."
Jason Lives: Friday the 13th Part VI	"Aladdin Sane"	The 2nd track on Bowie's 1973 album of the same name.
Friday the 13th Part VII: The New Blood	Birthday Bash	Title actually reflected part of the plot of the film. There was a birthday bash going on.
Friday the 13th Part VIII: Jason Takes Manhattan	"Ashes To Ashes"	The 4th track and first released song from Bowie's 1980 album "Scary Monsters (and Super Creeps)."

6-13

THE FIRST JASON

Answers on page 150

Here are some questions "submitted" by Ari Lehman, the First Jason. Most of these answers can be found elsewhere in this book – if you were paying attention.

1) Although better remembered for his role on *The Jeffersons* or in the film *The Warriors*, what actor had an uncredited role as a busboy in the opening scenes of the original *Friday the 13th*?
2) Though he currently plays a "machete keytar" in his band, First Jason, what other musical instrument and style did Ari Lehman study as a youth?
3) Which of First Jason's songs is used as a category title in this book?
4) What was the actual name of the pond in Camp No-Be-Bo-Sco, which was used as Crystal Lake in the original *Friday the 13th*?
5) Who composed the music for the original *Friday the 13th*, leading to him being credited in all but one of the original films of the series?
6) The production company responsible for *Friday the 13th* was based in what New England city and state?
7) For Ari Lehman's eight-second on-screen appearance, he had to endure how many hours in the special effects makeup chair?

"I think it would be more productive if we split up."
– Uncle Charles McCulloch (Friday the 13th Part VIII: Jason Takes Manhattan)

POP GOES THE WORLD

Answers on page 151

1) What magazine does Debbie read while waiting for Andy to return in *Friday the 13th Part 3*?
   a. *SCREAM*
   b. *People*
   c. *Fangoria*
   d. *Life*

2) To promote the premiere of *Friday the 13th Part VIII: Jason Takes Manhattan*, Kane Hodder appeared in full Jason costume on what late night talk show? (He didn't say a single word!)
   a. The Tonight Show with Johnny Carson
   b. Late Night with David Letterman
   c. The Arsenio Hall Show
   d. Later with Greg Kinnear

3) What is the company name on Lizabeth's credit card, which looks like an American Express card?
   a. American Express
   b. Master Express
   c. American Excess
   d. Banker's Express

4) What popular pinball machine can be seen in the background when some of the counselors go out to a bar in *Friday the 13th Part 2*?
   a. 8-Ball Deluxe
   b. KISS
   c. Black Knight
   d. Pinbot

5) What video game is Tommy Jarvis playing when we first see him in *Friday the 13th: The Final Chapter* (Part 4)?
   a. Defender
   b. Missile Command
   c. Centipede
   d. Zaxxon

6) *In Friday the 13th Part 3*, Chris's van has a bumper sticker for what popular musical artist?
   a. Bon Jovi
   b. Bruce Springsteen
   c. Billy Joel
   d. Gloria Gaynor

7) What movie were Robin and Jake watching in *Friday the 13th: A New Beginning*?
   a. *A Place in the Sun*
   b. *Ivanhoe*
   c. *BUtterfield 8*
   d. *Who's Afraid of Virginia Woolf?*

8) What popular catchphrase from another movie is said in *Jason Lives: Friday the 13th Part VI*?
   a. "I feel the need…the need for speed!"
   b. "I'll be back!"
   c. "I'm your density. I mean, your destiny."
   d. "No shirt, No shoes…No dice!"

9) What graduation gift does Rennie get from Mrs. Van Deusen in *Friday the 13th Part VIII: Jason Takes Manhattan*?
   a. 2 tickets to see *Cats* while in Manhattan
   b. A small easel once used by Pablo Picasso
   c. A pen used in high school by Stephen King
   d. An acoustic guitar once owned by Janis Joplin

10) What movie spoof of *Friday the 13th* starred Richard Benjamin, Paula Prentiss, and Jeffrey Tambor?

a. *The Final Terror*
b. *Saturday the 14th*
c. *Student Bodies*
d. *April Fools' Day*

11) The charm on the necklace that Sean gives to Rennie in *Friday the 13th Part VIII: Jason Takes Manhattan* is of what landmark?

a. Statue of Liberty
b. Carnegie Hall
c. Empire State Building
d. Yankee Stadium

12) In *Friday the 13th Part 2*, Terry wears a shirt that has what cartoon character on it?

a. Mickey Mouse
b. Mighty Mouse
c. Danger Mouse
d. Jerry Mouse

13) Ted in *The Final Chapter*, Violet in *A New Beginning*, and Cort in *Jason Lives* can all be seen with what staple of 1980s pop culture?

a. Rubik's Cube
b. Parachute pants
c. Sony Walkman
d. Members Only jacket

15) Matthew Letter, who runs Pinehurst in *Friday the 13th: A New Beginning*, has a book about mastering what video game on his desk?

a. Donkey Kong
b. Zaxxon
c. Centipede
d. Pac-Man

16) What other movie franchise is seen on Wade's shirt in the *Friday the 13th* reboot?

a. *Jaws*
b. *A Nightmare On Elm Street*
c. *The Evil Dead*
d. *Star Wars*

RELEASE THE HOUNDS!

There have been a few unnamed cats in the films, but the dogs almost always had names. Here are all of them.

Name	Breed	Owner	Film
Muffin	Shih Tzu mix	Terry	*Friday the 13th Part 2*
Gordon	Golden Retriever	Jarvis Family	*Friday the 13th: The Final Chapter*
Toby	Border Collie	Rennie Wickham	*Friday the 13th Part VIII: Jason Takes Manhattan*
Tango	Mutt	Stray fed by Diana Kimble	*Jason Goes to Hell: The Final Friday*
Unnamed	German Shepherd	Unnamed Old Lady	*Friday the 13th (2009)*

WELCOME BACK...

Other than Jason and Pamela Voorhees, and excluding dream sequences and archive footage, there have been only a few recurring characters in the films. Here they are.

<table>
<tr><th>Character</th><th>Films</th><th>Actor(s)</th></tr>
<tr><td>Alice Hardy</td><td rowspan="2">Friday the 13th, Friday the 13th Part 2</td><td>Adrienne King</td></tr>
<tr><td>Crazy Ralph</td><td>Walt Gorney</td></tr>
<tr><td>Tommy Jarvis</td><td>The Final Chapter, A New Beginning, Jason Lives</td><td>Corey Feldman, John Shepherd, Thom Mathews</td></tr>
</table>

TOMMY, CAN YOU HEAR ME?

Answers on page 152

Tommy Jarvis is in three straight films. Here are some questions all about Jason's most frequent adversary.

1) How old was Tommy Jarvis when we first meet him in *Friday the 13th: The Final Chapter*?
2) What is the name of the mental health facility that Tommy Jarvis lives at during the start of *Friday the 13th: A New Beginning*?
3) Corey Feldman was supposed to reprise his role as Tommy Jarvis in *Friday the 13th: A New Beginning*, but was too busy with the filming of what other movie?
4) Not counting dream sequences, besides Jason Voorhees, who is the only other person we see Tommy Jarvis kill?
5) What is the name of Tommy Jarvis's friend from the Unger Institute that goes to Jason's grave with him in *Jason Lives: Friday the 13th Part VI*?
6) Who did the blue pickup truck that Tommy Jarvis was driving in *Jason Lives: Friday the 13th Part VI* belong to originally?
7) Who was set to portray Tommy Jarvis in *Freddy vs. Jason* until the part was trimmed due to the length of the film?

"Dude, that goalie was pissed about something!"
– Bill Freeburg (Freddy vs. Jason)

VS. THE PAST

Answers on page 153

1) What is the name of the hospital where Will and Mark were patients, which was also the birthplace of Freddy Krueger?
2) Who had the idea of giving patients at the hospital the experimental drug Hypnocil, which suppresses dreams, in *A Nightmare On Elm Street Part 3: Dream Warriors*?
3) What were the call letters of the TV station seen at the hospital – the same letters as the radio station Glen Lantz was listening to right before being killed in the original *A Nightmare On Elm Street*?
4) Blake's early dream sequence in *Freddy vs. Jason* was a reference to whose dream in the original *A Nightmare On Elm Street*, which also involved a goat?
5) When Kia walks up to distract Freddy from killing Lori and Will in *Freddy vs. Jason*, what does Freddy say to her, a variation of a well-known line from *A Nightmare On Elm Street Part 4: The Dream Master*?
6) What was Freddy Krueger nicknamed before parents burned him to death?

JASON NEVER FORGETS

Answers on page 154

1) When Freddy cuts off Jason's fingers and Jason stares at his hand for a minute, it is copying a similar scene from which previous *Friday the 13th* film?
   a. *Part 3*
   b. *Part VIII: Jason Takes Manhattan*
   c. *Jason X*
   d. *The Final Chapter*

2) When the kids are ridiculing Jason in a dream sequence in *Freddy vs. Jason*, what do they do to him before pushing him in the water?
   a. Tape his mouth shut
   b. Put a sack over his head
   c. Strip him naked
   d. Hit him in the head with a hammer

3) Freddy drives his blades into Jason's eyes at one point, bringing back memories of which actress's kill in *Friday the 13th: A New Beginning*, when Roy (impersonating Jason) drove a pair of hedge trimming shears into her eyes?
   a. Jensen Daggett
   b. Lar Park-Lincoln
   c. Deborah Voorhees
   d. Amy Steel

4) When Jason killed Gibb and Frissell in a double impalement with a metal spike, it was copying a kill of what couple from *Friday the 13th Part 2*?
   a. Jeff and Sandra
   b. Shelly and Vera
   c. Jack and Marcie
   d. Cort and Nikki

6-13

HE'S GOT ISSUES

Answers on page 155

Through the years there have been a number of comic books starring everybody's favorite masked slasher, Jason Voorhees.

1) What other horror movie icon did Topps have Jason do battle with in a three-issue 1995 comic mini-series?
   a. Pinhead
   b. Leatherface
   c. Freddy Krueger
   d. Michael Myers

2) What was Mrs. Voorhees's name said to be in that 1995 comic book series?
   a. Pam
   b. Adrienne
   c. Marilyn
   d. Doris

3) Topps gave Jason a cameo appearance in what 1993 comic, which chronicled his passing through "limbo" after the events of *Jason Goes to Hell*?
   a. *Jason Meets Satan*
   b. *Jason Damned*
   c. *Satan's Six*
   d. *The Devil's Children*

4) What two other horror icons are pitted against Jason in a six-comic series titled *The Nightmare Warriors* in 2009?
   a. Freddy and Ash
   b. Freddy and Leatherface
   c. Freddy and Pinhead
   d. Leatherface and Michael Myers

GRAPHIC DETAILS

Comic Book Series	Manufacturer	Issues	First Issue Date
Jason Goes To Hell	Topps	3	1993
Satan's Six	Topps	1	1993
Jason vs. Leatherface	Topps	3	1995
Friday the 13th Special	Avatar	1	May 2005
Jason X Special	Avatar	1	October 2005
Jason vs. Jason X	Avatar	2	February 2006
Friday the 13th Fearbook	Avatar	1	June 2006
Friday the 13th Bloodbath	Avatar	3	September 2006
Friday the 13th 2007	WildStorm	6	December 6, 2006
Friday the 13th: Pamela's Tale 2007	WildStorm	2	July 11, 2007
Friday the 13th: How I Spent My Summer Vacation 2007	WildStorm	2	September 12, 2007
Freddy vs. Jason vs. Ash 2008	WildStorm	6	November 7, 2007
Friday the 13th: Bad Land 2008	WildStorm	2	January 9, 2008
Friday the 13th: Abuser and the Abused 2008	WildStorm	1	April 30, 2008
Freddy vs. Jason vs. Ash: The Nightmare Warriors 2009	WildStorm	6	June 24, 2009

6-13

PROPPING IT FORWARD

Answers on page 156

Some props that have appeared in *Friday the 13th* films were also used in other films. The majority of them made their appearance in *Jason Goes to Hell: The Final Friday.*

Match these props with their other films:

1) Jason's heart (Part 9)
2) Necronomicon (Part 9)
3) The Jarvis house (Part 4)
4) Metal jungle gym (Part 9)
5) Crate marked "Arctic Expedition" in the Voorhees's basement (Part 9)

a. *The Birds* (1963)
b. *Creepshow* (1982)
c. *The Evil Dead* (1981)
d. *Ed Gein* (2000)
e. *From Dusk Till Dawn* (1996)

6) Which actor got to kill Jason's heart from *Jason Goes To Hell: The Final Friday* in the other movie it appeared in?

7) The "Arctic Expedition" crate contained a creature when it was used in a film before *Jason Goes to Hell: The Final Friday*. What was the on-set nickname for the creature at that time?

HODDER THAN HELL

Answers on page 157

All of these questions pertain to the four movies starring Kane Hodder as Jason.

1) How many times do we see Kane Hodder get killed in *Jason Goes to Hell: The Final Friday*?

2) In *Friday the 13th Part VII: The New Blood*, who was the surprise birthday party supposed to be for?

3) Kane Hodder has said that his favorite moment of portraying Jason Voorhees was which of these?
   a. Standing in Times Square in full costume
   b. Falling through the steps in *The New Blood*
   c. Getting blown up in *Jason Goes to Hell*
   d. Emerging as Uber-Jason in *Jason X*

4) What is the name of the doctor that is helping Tina in *Friday the 13th Part VII: The New Blood*?

5) What is the name of the captain of the SS *Lazarus* in *Friday the 13th Part VIII: Jason Takes Manhattan*?

6) Which character in *Friday the 13th Part VIII: Jason Takes Manhattan* carries a video camera with him everywhere he goes?

7) What is the name of the coroner that eats Jason's heart in *Jason Goes to Hell: The Final Friday*?

8) What is the title of Kane Hodder's autobiography, which is subtitled *True Life Story Of The World's Most Prolific, Cinematic Killer*?

9) Who was the prom queen at Lakeview High School in *Friday the 13th Part VIII: Jason Takes Manhattan*?

10) What is the name of the bounty hunter that is after Jason in *Jason Goes to Hell: The Final Friday*?

11) Kane Hodder can be seen portraying Victor Crowley in the first three installments of what other horror movie?

12) Whose arm is chopped off when the cryogenically-frozen body of Jason falls over in *Jason X*?

13) What is the name of the android in *Jason X*?

14) Who is the pilot of the *Grendel* in *Jason X*?

15) Kane Hodder has said that his favorite kill from his time as Jason Voorhees was which of these kills?
    a. Dr. Crews cut in half with weed whacker
    b. Killing himself as the morgue security guard
    c. Swinging Judy in her sleeping bag into a tree
    d. Punching Julius's head off

"A few minor repairs and it'll be good as new."
– Shelly (Friday the 13th Part 3)

I'M DRIVING IN MY CAR

Answers on page 158

Match these automobiles to the character we mainly see driving them.

1) Dodge Ram Van
2) 1977 Chevy Camaro
3) Red Volkswagen convertible
4) Marlin Blue Ford F-100 Custom Cab pickup
5) 1965 Jeep CJ-5

   a. Megan Garris
   b. Pam Roberts
   c. Ginny Field
   d. Mrs. Pamela Voorhees
   e. Chris Higgins

6) What company manufactured the RV that belonged to Nikki's stepfather Horace in *Jason Lives: Friday the 13th Part VI*?

7) What type of vehicle is Trent driving in the *Friday the 13th* reboot?

8) In what month does the New Jersey state inspection expire on the Volkswagen that Shelly and Vera drive to the store in *Friday the 13th Part 3*, as can be noted by the sticker on the car's windshield?

9) What does it say on the hood of the van driven by Will Rollins in *Freddy vs. Jason*?

SURVIVAL GUIDE

Film	Survivors	Notes
Friday the 13th (1980)	Alice Hardy	Killed at the start of Part 2
Friday the 13th Part 2	Ginny Field Paul Holt	Paul's survival is in question.
Friday the 13th Part 3	Chris Higgins	
Friday the 13th: The Final Chapter	Trish Jarvis Tommy Jarvis	
Friday the 13th: A New Beginning	Pam Roberts Reggie Tommy Jarvis	
Jason Lives: Friday the 13th Part VI	Megan Garris Tommy Jarvis All the children	Tommy Jarvis never dies in the original films.
Friday the 13th Part VII: The New Blood	Tina Shepard Nick	
Friday the 13th Part VIII: Jason Takes Manhattan	Rennie Wickham Sean Robertson	
Jason Goes to Hell: The Final Friday	Jessica Kimble Steven Freeman Baby Stephanie	
Jason X	Rowan Tsunaron Kay-Em 14's head	
Freddy vs. Jason	Lori Campbell Will Rollins	
Friday the 13th (2009)	Clay Miller Whitney Miller	Great jump scene at the end pays tribute to the original.

THE ONE THING

Answers on page 159

Many numbers appear in the films. Here are a few of them.

1) Fan-Submitted Question from James Maxwell: In the original *Friday the 13th*, what number is on the canoe that can be seen before Mrs. Voorhees and Alice have their final fight that ends with Mrs. Voorhees's decapitation?
2) In which film is there a car with Alabama license plate #DKU-479?
3) What brand of gas is sold at the gas station and convenience store that Shelly and Vera go to in *Friday the 13th Part 3*?
4) Rennie, Sean, and Jason enter the subway at what numbered street and Broadway in *Friday the 13th Part VIII: Jason Takes Manhattan*?

Match these characters to the number that appeared on their shirts or jackets.

1) Mark (Part 2)	a. #8
2) Ted (Part 1)	b. #10
3) Reggie (Part 5)	c. #13
4) Shack (*vs.*)	d. #37
5) Sissy (Part 6)	e. #66
6) Azrael (*Jason X*)	f. #81
7) Stephen (Part 9)	g. #88

ROUNDABOUT (IN AND AROUND THE LAKE)

Answers on page 160

1) Who killed Joey at the start of *Friday the 13th: A New Beginning*?
   a. Tommy Jarvis
   b. Matthew Letter
   c. Victor J. Faden
   d. Roy the Paramedic
2) What does the Jarvis family call their family group hug?
   a. Trish Squish
   b. Jarvis Sandwich
   c. Bear Hug
   d. Wrap N Squeeze
3) The actor that formerly portrayed which character provided the opening narration for *Friday the 13th Part VII: The New Blood*?
   a. Crazy Ralph
   b. Paul Holt
   c. Tommy Jarvis
   d. Jack
4) What is the name of the investigative news show hosted by Robert Campbell in *Jason Goes to Hell: The Final Friday*?
   a. *In Depth*
   b. *American Case File*
   c. *In Search Of…*
   d. *The Crime Files*
5) Not counting the opening sequence archive footage of the previous films, what is the only *Friday the 13th* movie to never mention the name Jason?
   a. *Friday the 13th Part 2*
   b. *Friday the 13th: A New Beginning*
   c. *Jason X*
   d. *Friday the 13th Part 3*

6) What is the name of the Coast Guard ship that begins to respond to Sean's distress call in *Friday the 13th Part VIII: Jason Takes Manhattan*?
   a. CG Cutter *Dallas*
   b. CG Rescue *Trenton*
   c. CG Cutter *Omaha*
   d. CG Rescue *Bismarck*

7) What is the hitchhiker's destination, according to her sign, in *Friday the 13th: The Final Chapter*?
   a. Carnegie Hall or Bust
   b. Canada and Love
   c. Parsippany and Peace
   d. No Sleep 'Til Brooklyn

8) What message did Freddy burn into Mark's back in *Freddy vs. Jason*?
   a. Sleep Tight
   b. Jason Sucks
   c. I'm Coming For You
   d. Freddy's Back

9) Rennie was directly responsible for the death of which character in *Friday the 13th Part VIII: Jason Takes Manhattan*?
   a. Claudia Van Damme
   b. Colleen Van Deusen
   c. Bree Van De Kamp
   d. Jeannie Van Der Hooven

10) What items are set up like a sort of wind chime in Jason's cabin in the 2009 *Friday the 13th* reboot?
   a. Bones
   b. Keys
   c. Whistles
   d. Knives

11) The house the kids are staying at in *Friday the 13th Part VII: The New Blood* belongs to whose uncle?
   a. Russell
   b. Eddie
   c. Nick
   d. Tina

12) In what city and state is the Federal Morgue that Jason's remains are sent to at the start of *Jason Goes to Hell: The Final Friday*?

a. Youngstown, OH
b. Scranton, PA
c. Saugerties, NY
d. Baltimore, MD

13) What message does Paul Holt leave in the fogged up mirror for Ginny after they spent the night together in *Friday the 13th Part 2*?

a. Love Ya
b. Jason Lives
c. Beware of Bears
d. PH+GF in a heart

14) What is the name of the restaurant and coffee shop in *Jason Goes to Hell: The Final Friday*?

a. Shelby's
b. Do-Bee's
c. Joey B's
d. Aunt Bea's

15) What unusual weapon does Linderman stab Jason with in *Freddy vs. Jason*?

a. Golf club
b. Camera tripod
c. U.S. flag on a pole
d. Chair leg

16) What is the name of the female FBI agent used as bait at the beginning of *Jason Goes to Hell: The Final Friday*?

a. Elizabeth Marcus
b. Pamela Hardy
c. Dana Scully
d. Sandra Dyer

17) What is the name of the boat that Jim and Suzy are on when Jason wakes up at the bottom of Crystal Lake in *Friday the 13th Part VIII: Jason Takes Manhattan*?

a. *Lady Liberty*
b. *Lazarus Lady*
c. *Lady Drifter*
d. *Lady of the Lake*

18) What was Reggie's nickname in *Friday the 13th: A New Beginning*?
   a. Running Reggie
   b. Spider-Man
   c. Reggie the Reckless
   d. Mr. October

19) How much money does Creighton Duke want to kill Jason in *Jason Goes to Hell: The Final Friday*?
   a. $250,000
   b. $500,000
   c. $1,000,000
   d. $5,000,000

20) What video game system was the 1989 *Friday the 13th* video game made for?
   a. Nintendo (NES)
   b. Sega
   c. Atari 9600
   d. Sony Playstation

21) In the 1989 video game *Friday the 13th*, when you encountered Jason in a cabin, he would fight you in the style of what other popular video game?
   a. Street Fighter
   b. Punch Out
   c. Krull
   d. Mortal Kombat

22) What is the physical manifestation of Jason Voorhees's soul called in *Jason Goes to Hell: The Final Friday*?
   a. Jason XY
   b. Hellbaby
   c. The Thing
   d. Head

23) Which character in *Friday the 13th Part VIII: Jason Takes Manhattan* plays the guitar?
   a. Charles McCulloch
   b. C.C. DeVille
   c. Miles Wolfe
   d. J.J. Jarrett

EVERY PICTURE TELLS A STORY

Through the years there have been many novelizations and other books based on the films. Here is a list of them all.

Book Title	Author, Publisher	Year
Novelizations		
Friday the 13th Part 3	Michael Avallone, Tower & Leisure Sales Co.	1982
Friday the 13th Part VI: Jason Lives	Simon Hawke, Signet	1986
Friday the 13th	Simon Hawke, Signet	1987
Friday the 13th Part 2	Simon Hawke, Signet	1988
Friday the 13th Part 3	Simon Hawke, Signet	1989
Freddy vs. Jason	Stephen Hand, Black Flame	2003
Jason X	Pat Cadigan, Black Flame	2005
Camp Crystal Lake Series		
Friday the 13th: Mother's Day	Eric Morse, Berkley Books	1994
Friday the 13th: Jason's Curse	Eric Morse, Berkley Books	1994
Friday the 13th: The Carnival	Eric Morse, Berkley Books	1994
Friday the 13th: Road Trip	Eric Morse, Berkley Books	1994
Jason X Series		
Jason X: The Experiment	Pat Cadigan, Black Flame	2005
Jason X: Planet of the Beast	Nancy Kilpatrick, Black Flame	2005
Jason X: Death Moon	Alex Johnson, Black Flame	2005
Jason X: To the Third Power	Nancy Kilpatrick, Black Flame	2006
Friday the 13th Series		
Church of the Divine Psychopath	Scott Phillips, Black Flame	2005
Hell Lake	Paul A. Woods, Black Flame	2005
Hate-Kill-Repeat	Jason Arnopp, Black Flame	2005
The Jason Strain	Christ Faust, Black Flame	2006
Carnival of Maniacs	Stephen Hand, Black Flame	2006

DIRECTOR'S SLASH

Answers on page 161

1) What was the first film in which Sean S. Cunningham directed Ari Lehman, the First Jason?
2) Steve Miner, who directed *Friday the 13th Part 2* and *Part 3*, directed which film from the *Halloween* movie franchise?
3) Joseph Zito directed *Friday the 13th: The Final Chapter,* which opened at #1 in the U.S. box office. What two films, which also opened at #1 in the U.S., did he direct after that, making three straight #1-openers?
4) *Friday the 13th: A New Beginning* director Danny Steinmann got the job after plans for a sequel to what 1972 horror film fell through, a sequel he was set to direct?
5) *Jason Lives: Friday the 13th Part VI* director Tom McLoughlin keeps what prop from the film in his backyard?
6) *Jason Goes to Hell: The Final Friday* director Adam Marcus wrote the story and screenplay for what 3-D sequel remake in 2013?
7) *Freddy vs. Jason* director Ronny Yu directed which film in the *Child's Play* movie franchise?
8) *Friday the 13th* reboot director Marcus Nispel has also directed what two other franchise reboots?

6-13

ALL IN THE FAMILY

Some *Friday the 13th* alumni also have some famous relatives.

Actor	Famous Parent
Harry Crosby: Bill in *Friday the 13th (1980)*	Father - Bing Crosby (Musician and actor: *Holiday Inn*, *Road To . . .* films with Bob Hope)
Kimberly Beck: Trish Jarvis in *The Final Chapter*	Father - Tommy Leonetti (Actor: *Gomer Pyle USMC*, *Massacre at Central High*)
Crispin Glover: Jimbo in *The Final Chapter*	Father - Bruce Glover (Actor: *Chinatown*, *Diamonds Are Forever*)
Tiffany Helm: Violet in *A New Beginning*	Mother - Brooke Bundy (Actress: *A Nightmare on Elm Street* 3 and 4)
Tony Goldwyn: Darren in *Jason Lives*	Grandfather – Samuel Goldwyn (Producer)
Tom Fridley: Cort in *Jason Lives*	Mother – Ellen Travolta (Actress: *Charles in Charge*, *Happy Days* - both as Scott Baio's mom. Sister of John Travolta)
Jason Ritter: Will Rollins in *Freddy vs. Jason*	Father – John Ritter (Actor: *Three's Company*, *8 Simple Rules*, so much more)

STAGE FRIGHT

Answers on page 162

1) Which *Friday the 13th* franchise cast member was Miss Florida and a runner-up in the 1978 Miss America Pageant?

2) Which *Friday the 13th* leading lady was once a contestant on the TV game show *Scrabble* as a teenager?

3) Which actress, who portrayed Vicki in *Jason Goes to Hell: The Final Friday*, had previously portrayed Allie's daughter Jennie Lowell on the TV sit-com *Kate & Allie*?

4) Actor Lawrence Monoson's (Ted in *The Final Chapter*) first role was as Gary in what 1982 coming-of-age story?

5) Shavar Ross, who portrayed Reggie in *Friday the 13th: A New Beginning*, portrayed what 1980s sit-com character's best friend?

6) What *Friday the 13th* actress was Miss Teen USA 1985 and once portrayed the love interest of Kirk Cameron's character Mike Seaver on the TV show *Growing Pains*?

7) What *Friday the 13th* leading lady gave up acting soon after her battle with Jason and now helps her husband Mo Siegel run the Celestial Seasons tea brand he founded?

8) Which former Sweathog was in a *Friday the 13th* film?

9) Judie Aronson went on to portray Hilly, who was Deb's best friend, in what 1985 John Hughes film?

10) Jennifer Banko, who portrayed Tina Shepard as a child in the opening flashback of *Friday the 13th Part VII: The New Blood,* went on to play what other horror movie main character's daughter in a 1990 sequel?

11) William Butler, who portrayed the birthday boy Michael in *Friday the 13th Part VII: The New Blood*, went on to write the story for which horror movie and its two sequels?

12) *Jason X* co-stars Lexa Doig and Lisa Ryder were also co-stars of what 2000-2005 syndicated TV series?

13) Which *Friday the 13th* actor would go on to the recurring movie role of Bernie Lomax?

14) Actor Peter Mensah portrayed Oenomaus on what Starz original series?

15) *Freddy vs. Jason* co-stars Jason Ritter and Chris Marquette also co-starred in what 2003-2005 TV series about the Girardi family and God?

16) Which member of Destiny's Child has portrayed a major character in a *Friday the 13th* film?

17) What *Friday the 13th* actor was badly burned when a stunt went wrong on the set of the TV show *The Powers Of Matthew Star*, which shut down production for a year while he healed?

"Hey, you want a beer? Or to smoke some pot? Or we could have pre-marital sex. We love pre-marital sex!"
– Two Holographic Female Campers (Jason X)

JASON X-RATED

Answers on page 163

1) Which *Friday the 13th* film director was formerly an adult film director?
2) *Which Friday the 13th: A New Beginning* actress formerly worked as a Playboy Bunny at a Playboy Club?
3) In *Jason X*, Tsunaron is trying to add what upgrade to his android Kay-Em 14, at her request?
4) Actress Darcy DeMoss, who portrayed Nikki in *Jason Lives: Friday the 13th Part VI*, had previously appeared on what TV show in *The Final Chapter*, which was being watched by one of the characters?
5) Which character was killed while watching old black and white stag/burlesque films?
6) Which *Friday the 13th* film had the most nudity?
7) What is the only *Friday the 13th* film that has absolutely no nudity in it?
8) Who purchased a box of condoms while at Outpost in the *Friday the 13th* reboot?

9) What magazine is Shelly reading in the store when Vera asks him for money in *Friday the 13th Part 3*?

10) What magazine is Donnie reading in the barn shortly before he is killed in *Friday the 13th* (2009)?

11) In an attempt to keep up with real-world events in the movies, which two characters can be seen making a sex tape in the 2009 *Friday the 13th* reboot?

12) How did Jason's "Hellbaby" make its way into the body of Diana Kimble, which allowed Jason to be reborn?

13) Which of the twins did Jimbo have sex with in *Friday the 13th: The Final Chapter*?

14) Through the years there has been a lot of nudity in the *Friday the 13th* films. Which female character was the first to be shown topless?

15) What producer walked out of the 2009 reboot movie premiere because he felt it had too much sex in it?

16) Who has been the hostess of the Playboy Channel's "Playboy's Home Shopping" program?

17) What board game do counselors Alice, Bill, and Brenda play a strip version of in Part 1?

18) Which actress from the *Friday the 13th* reboot was not only Playboy Magazine's February 2000 Babe of the Month, but is also Neve Campbell's sister-in-law?

COULD'VE BEEN

Some other actors and directors nearly made it into the *Friday the 13th* franchise. Here are some of the more notable ones.

Person	Role	Notes
Sally Field	Alice Hardy	Auditioned
Elizabeth Berkley	Rennie Wickham	Auditioned
Dedee Pfeiffer	Rennie Wickham	Auditioned
Tobe Hooper	Director candidate: *Jason Goes to Hell: The Final Friday*	Directed *The Texas Chainsaw Massacre* and *Poltergeist*
John McTiernan	Offered the directing job for *Jason Goes to Hell: The Final Friday*	Directed *Last Action Hero*, *Die Hard*, and *Predator*.
Jason Bateman	Was set to portray Tommy Jarvis in *Freddy vs. Jason*	The script was too long; the role was written out.
Rob Zombie	Offered the directing job for *Freddy vs. Jason*	Directed his own *House of 1000 Corpses* instead.
Brad Renfro	Will Rollins	Replaced due to drug-related issues; Jason Ritter took over.
Steve Norrington	Offered the directing job for *Freddy vs. Jason*	Directed *Blade*; did effects for *Aliens* and *Alien 3*
Scout Taylor-Compton	Jenna	Auditioned
Samuel Bayer	Turned down the directing job for the reboot	Directed the *A Nightmare On Elm Street* reboot

BEHIND THE SCENES

Answers on page 164

1) What name is used for Jason in the scripts during auditioning so that actors do not know it is a *Friday the 13th* film?
   a. Ralph
   b. Jacob
   c. Ethan
   d. Eddie
2) What was the final film done by Paramount Pictures before New Line Cinema took over the franchise?
   a. *Part VII: The New Blood*
   b. *Part VIII: Jason Takes Manhattan*
   c. *Jason Goes to Hell: The Final Friday*
   d. *Jason X*
3) What was Jason's name originally going to be?
   a. Ethan
   b. Josh
   c. Frankie
   d. Ritchie
4) Franchise creator Sean S. Cunningham wanted to make *Friday the 13th* after seeing the success of what other horror movie?
   a. *Dawn of the Dead*
   b. *The Hills Have Eyes*
   c. *The Texas Chainsaw Massacre*
   d. *Halloween*
5) What was the only building/locale that had to be built in Camp Crystal Lake for the original *Friday the 13th*?
   a. Alice's cabin
   b. The bathroom
   c. The archery range
   d. The lake

6) Which crew member doubled as Brenda's dead body when it is thrown through the window in the original *Friday the 13th*?
   a. Kevin Bacon
   b. Ari Lehman
   c. Tom Savini
   d. Sean S. Cunningham

7) Tom Savini came up with the idea for the scene where Jason pulls Alice into the lake because he felt the movie needed a "chair jumper" moment like he had recently seen in which horror movie?
   a. *Carrie*
   b. *The Shining*
   c. *Jaws*
   d. *The Amityville Horror*

8) One early concept for *Jason Goes to Hell: The Final Friday* was to have Jason continue his travels, this time to what city?
   a. Las Vegas
   b. Niagara Falls
   c. Miami
   d. Los Angeles

9) After that idea was scrapped, what was the title of *Jason Goes to Hell: the Final Friday* going to be?
   a. *Friday the 13th Part IX: Family Ties*
   b. *Friday the 13th Part IX: The F.B.I. Files*
   c. *Friday the 13th Part IX: The Dark Heart of Jason Voorhees*
   d. *The Final Friday: Laid to Rest*

10) Betsy Palmer took the role of Mrs. Pamela Voorhees because she needed the money to replace what item?
  a. Car
  b. House
  c. Swimming pool
  d. Her SAG card

11) Henry Manfredini did the score for the original movie and came up with that famous sound that lets us know the killer is nearby; what is actually said in that sound?
  a. "Chi-Chi- Chi, Ha-Ha-Ha"
  b. "Ki-Ki-Ki, Ma-Ma-Ma"
  c. "Shh-Shh-Shh, Ma-Ma-Ma"
  d. "Ma-Ma-Ma, Ha-Ha-Ha"

12) Director Ronny Yu says that how many gallons of fake blood were used during the filming of *Freddy vs. Jason*?
  a. 100 Gallons
  b. 200 Gallons
  c. 300 Gallons
  d. 500 Gallons

13) In the original *Friday the 13th*, which actor's death scene had a prop malfunction that necessitated one of the effects guys blowing into the blood tube, resulting in the cool blood spurting in the scene?
  a. Walt Gorney
  b. Betsy Palmer
  c. Harry Crosby
  d. Kevin Bacon

14) Willa Ford was given just ten days to learn what for the *Friday the 13th* reboot?
   a. Wakeboarding
   b. Surfing
   c. Swimming
   d. Driving

15) Corey Feldman's scene at the start *of Friday the 13th: A New Beginning* were shot in what location?
   a. Camp No-Be-Bo-Sco
   b. In his backyard
   c. On the set of *The Goonies*
   d. Los Angeles County Cemetery

16) What was co-creator Victor Miller's working title for the script for the original *Friday the 13th*?
   a. *Camp Crystal Lake*
   b. *Massacre at the Lake*
   c. *Long Night at Camp Blood*
   d. *Summer Camp Massacre*

17) *Jason X* writer Todd Farmer named many of the characters in the film after his friends in what online PC game?
   a. World of Warcraft
   b. Dragon Quest X
   c. AdventureQuest Worlds
   d. EverQuest

6-13

"It's gonna take more than a poke in the ribs to put down this old dog . . . yeah, that oughta do it"
– Sgt. Brodski (Jason X)

THE FINAL CUT

They've tried to kill Jason Voorhees in seven of the twelve films. Here is how he was left for dead.

Film	Killer	Means of Death
Friday the 13th Part 3	Chris Higgins	Axe to the head
Friday the 13th: The Final Chapter	Tommy Jarvis	Hacked repeatedly with the machete
Jason Lives: Friday the 13th Part VI	Tommy Jarvis and Megan Garris	Set on fire, chained to a boulder, sent to the bottom of Forest Green Lake, and hit with the blade from the boat motor
Friday the 13th Part VII: The New Blood	Mr. Shepard	Pulled him back down into Crystal Lake
Friday the 13th Part VIII: Jason Takes Manhattan	Rennie Wickham and Sean Robertson	Escaped Jason, who was trapped in the NYC sewer system when it filled with toxic waste at midnight
Jason Goes to Hell: The Final Friday	Jessica Kimble	Magic Dagger to the heart
Friday the 13th (2009)	Whitney Miller	Machete through the heart

THIS IS THE END

Answers on page 165

1) Fan-Submitted Question from Alan Clague: At the end of which two *Friday the 13th* films do we see Jason's mask floating on its own to the bottom of a lake?
2) Who is seen jumping from the water to pull Chris out of the boat at the end of *Friday the 13th Part 3*?
3) Who finally stops Jason at the end of *Friday the 13th Part VII: The New Blood*?
4) What two things is Jason carrying when he emerges from Crystal Lake at the end of *Freddy vs. Jason*?
5) Who are Rennie and Sean reunited with at the end of *Friday the 13th Part VIII: Jason Takes Manhattan*?
6) What drags Jason's mask to hell at the end of *Jason Goes to Hell: The Final Friday*?
7) At the end of *Jason X*, a couple on Earth II believe that Jason and Brodski entering the planet's atmosphere is what?
8) What two items do Clay and Whitney drop into the lake along with Jason's body?

6-13

FRIDAY THE 13TH: THE FINAL TALLY

Box office numbers are Domestic Lifetime Gross numbers. Budgets numbers are the accepted estimates.

Film	**Budget**	**Box Office**
Friday the 13th	$550,000	$39,754,601
Friday the 13th Part 2	$1,250,000	$21,722,776
Friday the 13th Part 3	$4,000,000	$36,690,067
Friday the 13th: The Final Chapter	$1,800,000	$32,980,880
Friday the 13th: A New Beginning	$2,200,000	$21,930,418
Jason Lives: Friday the 13th Part VI	$3,000,000	$19,472,057
Friday the 13th Part VII: The New Blood	$2,800,000	$19,170,001
Friday the 13th Part VIII: Jason Takes Manhattan	$5,000,000	$14,343,976
Jason Goes to Hell: The Final Friday	$2,500,000	$15,935,068
Jason X	$11,000,000	$13,121,555
Freddy vs. Jason	$25,000,000	$82,622,655
Friday the 13th (2009)	$19,000,000	$65,002,019
Totals	**$78,100,000**	**$382,746,073**

TIMELINES

If you were to go looking for a *Friday the 13th* timeline online, you would find a hundred different versions of it. I studied the majority of them! Some of them I just don't see how they come up with what they do. Many don't even have the right number of days, which is something rather easy to figure out.

Here is my version of the timeline. I think it is the most accurate and logical timeline you will find. Of course, I am sure many will disagree.

My timeline uses only ACTUAL calendar dates that exist, with one exception: the very first date of June 13, 1979. It just doesn't exist as a Friday. I think that is why they changed it in the reboot to 1980, because there is indeed a Friday, June 13th in 1980. Every other date I used has happened, with the obvious exception of 2455. With the exception of Parts 2-4, my timeline assumes that the bulk of the killing in the films takes place ON Friday the 13th.

Resources I used to come up with this timeline include, but are not limited to: many online timelines, some of the *Friday the 13th* books, the actual movies themselves, and a bit of common sense.

Examples:

In the Part VI novel, it says Tommy Jarvis was institutionalized for ten years total. This means when he heads to the cemetery with Hawes, he is 22 years old. This also means that *Jason Lives* should take place in 1994. When you look at the 1994 calendar, the only time kids might be arriving at camp near a Friday the 13th is in May.

In *A New Beginning*, you can clearly see an October calendar outside Violet's room right before Jake gets a cleaver to the head, so the film doesn't take place in May! If it took place on October 13th, look at the calendar again and your options are 1989 or 1995. Only 1989 really works.

Also, you can't base timelines on how old an actor was in the film. I saw many people doing this. If you did that, Jason would have been 57 in *The Final Chapter*!

Take it or leave it, here is my timeline. I am 98% certain of accuracy in the first four films, and am slightly less certain on Parts V and VI. Parts VII and VII get a little iffy (several presumptions must be made); Part IX is a bit of a craps shoot; *Jason X* couldn't tell you in the movie what their timeline was; and *Freddy vs. Jason* is fit in where it makes sense.

6-13

Friday the 13th

<u>Friday, June 13, 1979</u>: All the killing is done.

<u>Saturday, June 14, 1979</u>: Mrs. Voorhees is beheaded and Alice is found in the canoe.

It is widely believed that the first two films were set on July 13 because the only summer 13ths that were Fridays in 1979 and 1984 were in July. This is NOT true, despite the calendar. Mrs. Voorhees specifically tells us that it is Jason's birthday in Part 1, making it June 13, 1979.

Friday the 13th Part 2

<u>August 1979</u>: Alice's kill

<u>Thursday, July 12, 1984</u>: Counselors arrive and Crazy Ralph is killed.

<u>Friday, July 13, 1984</u>: The majority of the killing happens.

<u>Saturday, July 14, 1984</u>: Ginny is carted off in an ambulance.

I will concede that Part 2 was set in July since there is no true evidence to state otherwise. However, it HAS to be July 12, 13, and14; Tommy Jarvis reads a headline in *The Final Chapter*, which refers to Jason as "The Friday the 13th Killer." Why would they call him that if he didn't do the bulk of his first killing on the 13th?

Friday the 13th Part 3

Summer day in 1982: Chris flashes back to this date.

Saturday, July 14, 1984: The store owner, Harold, and his wife, Edna, are killed.

Sunday, July 15, 1984: Chris and her friends arrive at Higgins Haven. The bulk of the killing is done this day.

Monday, July 16, 1984: Chris is rescued this morning.

This film picks up the same day Ginny was carted off to the hospital. Chris states that she hasn't been to Higgins Haven in two years since her encounter with Jason. Since the movie takes place in 1984, Chris's encounter had to be in 1982.

Friday the 13th: The Final Chapter

Monday, July 16, 1984: Jason's body is taken to the morgue. Axel and a nurse are killed.
Tuesday, July 17, 1984: The teens who rent out the house next door to the Jarvises arrive.
Wednesday, July 18, 1984: The teens go skinny dipping during the day, and the majority of the murders happen during the night.

Trish is awake in the hospital in the final scene. For this to happen, the final scene had to occur sometime after midnight, making it Thursday, July 19. Unfortunately, there is no way to confirm this.

Friday the 13th: A New Beginning

Wednesday, October 11, 1989: Tommy arrives at Pinehurst. Joey, Pete, and Vinnie are killed.

Thursday, October 12, 1989: Billy and Lana are killed outside the diner.

Friday, October 13, 1989: Most of the killing happens on this day.

Tommy's wakeup/dream sequence in the hospital is most likely after midnight, making it Saturday, October 14. A shot of a calendar outside of Violet's room earlier in the film clearly says October. This means the year was either 1989 or 1995. In 1989, Tommy has been in the institution for 5 years, which makes him 17.

Jason Lives: Friday the 13th Part VI

Thursday, May 12, 1994: Hawes and two counselors, Darren and Lizabeth, are killed.

Friday, May 13, 1994: The majority of the killing took place this day.

Saturday, May 14, 1994: Briefly, Jason is seen underwater.

Tommy is now 22 years old. The Part VI novel states that he was in the mental institutions for 10 years. This would mean it is 1994. If you look at the actual calendar, the only Friday the 13th that year is in May.

Friday the 13th Part VII: The New Blood

Friday, October 13, 1995: Tina kills her dad.

Thursday, September 12, 2002: Tina and her mom arrive at the lake house for the first time since her dad's death. Tina awakens Jason. A surprise party is held next door. A few people are killed in the woods.

Friday, September 13, 2002: The majority of the killing happens this night. Jason is dragged back into the lake by Mr. Shepard, Tina's dad.

Saturday, September 14, 2002: Tina and Nick are taken away in an ambulance.

At the beginning of this film, Jason is chained at the bottom of the lake where Tommy left him. He is also mostly intact. If you look at the actual calendar, the next year, 1995, has a Friday, October 13th as seen on Tina's calendar in the flashback.

Tina is supposed to be 17, and it is feasible she was around 10 in the flashback. Visit the actual calendar and you have September 13, 2002.

6-13

Friday the 13th Part VIII: Jason Takes Manhattan

2000: 14-year-old Rennie gets a swimming lesson from Uncle Charles.

June 2003: The actual date is unclear. A DJ says they will be graduating on the 13th, not that they will be graduating tomorrow. One could assume, though, that it is the 12th. Jim and Suzy are killed.

Friday, June 13, 2003: They would have had to graduate early in the day, and then head to the Lazarus. Most of the killings happen on this night.

Saturday, June 14, 2003: Sean and Rennie live happily ever after as dawn approaches.

Part VIII is said to take place later in the same year as Part VII. However, it would be impossible for them to graduate between September and December 2002. It may take place in the same school year, perhaps, but not the same calendar year. Lakeview High School graduates on Friday the 13th. This moves us to June 13, 2003.

Jason Goes to Hell: The Final Friday

2005: Unknown day when Jason is blown up and autopsied.

Creighton Duke is interviewed a week later and claims that Jason is still alive.

A week after the interview, five more murders are committed, in Jason's style, between Youngstown and Crystal Lake.

If the main kill day was the 13th, then the above events happened in late April and early May.

Thursday, May 12, 2005: Diana is killed, along with 3 campers.

Friday, May 13, 2005: The majority of the killing takes place. Jessica uses the Magic Dagger to send Jason to Hell.

Saturday May 14, 2005: Jessica and Stephen walk off into the sunrise.

Robert Campbell says, "For over 20 years, the mere mention of the name "Jason Voorhees" has been enough to send a shudder of fear through the hearts of an entire nation." Do the math. This means the film took place AFTER 2004, which would be the 20th anniversary of his first known kills.

A comic book bridged the gap between Part VIII and this film. In it, the FBI trail Jason from Manhattan to Crystal Lake, where they set up the sting operation shown at the beginning of this film.

Jason X

<u>Friday, August 13, 2010</u>: Jason breaks free of his chains and kills Dr. Wimmer and six soldiers. He is then cryogenically frozen.

<u>2455</u> in space.

It is said that Rowan was in stasis for 4.55 centuries (455 years). That would mean she went into stasis in 2000. However, she herself talks about events that happened in 2008 and 2010.

This film can't remedy its own timeline. It therefore doesn't easily fit into the overall timeline. However, if they caught and started executing Jason in 2008, that means all the other films had to happen prior to that, including *Freddy vs. Jason.*

Freddy vs. Jason

<u>Thursday, October 12, 2007</u>: Freddy brings Jason back from Hell. Jason then kills three people.

<u>Friday, October 13, 2007</u>: The majority of the action and kills happen.

<u>Saturday, October 14, 2007</u>: Jason emerges from the lake with his machete in one hand and Freddy's live head in the other.

In the scene outside of the school the day after Jason's first murders, it is clearly fall. The film had to take place in either 2006 or 2007. The only fall 13th is October 2007.

Friday the 13th (2009)

Friday, June 13, 1980: Mrs. Voorhees is beheaded.

Listed as present day:

Day 1: Whitney and four friends hike in in search of the marijuana plants that supposedly grow wild near Camp Crystal Lake. That night, they are all killed. Later, it is revealed that Whitney survived.

Day 2 (six weeks later): Jenna and her friends arrive at the lake. Whitney's brother, Clay, arrives in search of Whitney. The majority of the murders take place this night.

Day 3: Clay and Whitney return Jason to the lake.

The date shown at the start is June 13, 1980. This date actually exists! This is why the timelines must remain separate.

After that initial 1980 event, no one can definitively say what year the events take place. Wade says, "The camp was closed like 20 years ago." This would put present day events in 2000. I believe, however, that he was meant to say almost 30 years ago to put the events in the year of the film, 2009.

I am pretty certain that Trent's car, an Escalade, was not a 2000 model, which suggests 2009 is "present day." In 2009, there were Friday the 13ths in February, March, and November. It could also be argued that since the film was released in February 2009, the date in question is near June 13, 2008.

KILL INDEX

KILL INDEX

Total kills listed by killer

Killer (Original 11 films)	Number of Kills (202 total)
Jason Voorhees*	150
Roy	17
Mrs. Pamela Voorhees	9
Alice Hardy, Vic Faden, Tommy Jarvis, Tina Shepard, Wayne Webber, Rennie Wickham, Jessica Kimble, Stephen Freeman, Freddy Krueger	1 (Each was responsible for one kill)
Dream Sequence Jason Voorhees**	5
Dream Sequence Tommy Jarvis***	1
Holograms killed by Jason Voorhees**	4
Self-kills****	3
Hull Breach	4
Reboot Kills (14 total)	
Jason Voorhees	13
Unnamed counselor (Alice Hardy)	1

*Includes kills while he possessed these characters and these three who died when he left their bodies:

- Coroner Phil: 12
- Deputy Josh: 1
- Robert Campbell: 8

** Not counted in Jason's total

*** Not counted in Tommy Jarvis's total

**** Self-kills were all in *Jason X*: two sacrificing themselves, one accidentally crashing a shuttle.

KILL INDEX

Friday the 13th (1980)

Character	Means of Death	Notes
Killer – Mrs. Pamela Voorhees (9)		
Barry	Hunting knife to stomach	1958 camp counselor
Claudette	Hunting knife to throat	1958 camp counselor; unseen kill
Annie Phillips	Throat slit with hunting knife	New cook at Camp Crystal Lake. Hitched a ride with Mrs. Voorhees.
Ned Rubenstein	Throat slit	Unseen kill
Jack Marand	Hand on head from behind, harpoon pushed up through bed into throat	Kevin Bacon's character.
Marcie Cunningham	Axe to head in bathroom	
Brenda	Unknown	Body thrown through window to confirm kill
Steve Christie	Stabbed in stomach with butcher knife	
Bill	Throat slit	Mounted to door of generator cabin with four arrows; unseen kill
Killer – Alice Hardy (1)		
Mrs. Pamela Voorhees	Decapitated with machete	

KILL INDEX

Friday the 13th Part 2 (1981)

Character	Means of Death	Notes
Killer: Jason (9)		
Alice	Icepick to the temple	Lone survivor of Part 1; killed in her apartment
Crazy Ralph	Wire around neck, strangled against a tree	Actor Walt Gorney would return to narrate the opening sequence of *Friday the 13th Part VII: The New Blood*
Deputy Winslow	Claw hammer to back of the head	Was the first to find the shrine to Mrs. Voorhees's head
Scott	Throat slit with machete	
Terry	Unknown	Unseen kill. Her body can later be seen next to the shrine to confirm
Mark	Machete to the face	Wheelchair then rolled back off the porch and down a flight of steps
Jeff	Both speared through the stomach, from the top as they were having sex.	
Sandra		
Vickie	Stabbed with butcher knife	

KILL INDEX

Friday the 13th Part 3 (1982)

Character	Means of Death	Notes
Killer – Jason (12 plus 1 unborn child)		
Harold	Cleaver to the chest	The storeowner
Edna	Knitting needle to the back of the neck	The storeowner's wife
Fox	Hung in the barn, pitchfork in the neck	Female motorcycle gang member
Loco	Pitchfork to stomach	Motorcycle gang member #2
Vera	Shot in the eye with a harpoon gun	First kill by Jason with the hockey mask on
Andy	Walking on his hands, machete to the crotch which split him in two	Scene had to be cut down to avoid an X rating.
Debbie and her unborn child	Machete up through a hammock into her stomach	Debbie refused to eat the marijuana in the van because she is pregnant.
Shelly	Throat slit	Unseen kill. Killed prior to Vera, but not confirmed until later when Chili sees him
Chuck	Shoved backwards and his hand goes into an electrical box, electrocuted	First electrocution

6-13

Character	**Means of Death**	**Notes**
Chili	Hot fire poker to her stomach	
Rick	Head squeezed until his eyeball flew out	
Ali	Hacked to death with machete	Leader of the motorcycle gang

KILL INDEX

Friday the 13th: The Final Chapter (1984)

Character	Means of Death	Notes
Killer – Jason (13)		
Axel	Throat slit with hacksaw, head spun backwards	Coroner at the hospital Jason is taken to
Nurse R. Morgan RN	Stabbed in chest, knife dragged down to stomach	
Unnamed female hitchhiker	Knife through back of neck	
Samantha	Knife through raft into stomach	Judie Aronson was submerged (except for her head)and it was very cold. Ted White threatened to walk off the film if the director didn't let her get out, as this scene took quite a bit of time to shoot and reshoot. Her lips turning blue was when the director finally let her go warm up.
Paul	Harpoon gun to crotch, then lifted and fired	
Terri	Impaled with spear-like implement	

6-13

Character	Means of Death	Notes
Mrs. Jarvis	Unknown	Unseen kill. Trish finds her body in a deleted scene
Jimbo	Corkscrew through hand into counter, cleaver to the face	
Tina	Thrown out 2nd story window onto a station wagon	
Ted	Butcher knife through movie screen into back of neck	Lawrence Monoson smoked marijuana for the first time before shooting his death scene.
Doug	Head squished against the bathroom wall	Ted White demanded that padding be added between Peter Barton and the bathroom wall due to a previous on-set injury.
Sarah	Double-sided axe	Thrown through door into her chest
Rob	Hacked at repeatedly with a hand rake	Funniest kill scene in the films; screams, "Help! He's killing me! He's killing me!"

KILL INDEX

Friday the 13th: A New Beginning (1985)

Character	Means of Death	Notes
Killer – Vic (1)		
Joey	Axe to the back repeatedly	Joey was Roy's son.
Killer – Roy in blue marked hockey mask (17)		
Vinnie	Lit flare shoved in mouth	Pete and Vinnie were in no other scenes. I believe they were just thrown in to fulfill the orders that director Danny Steinmann had of having a shock, scare, or kill scene every 8 minutes or so.
Pete	Throat slit from back seat of car with machete	
Billy	Axe to the back of the head	
Lana	Axe to the stomach	Lana gets lumped in with Pete and Vinnie above. There was an unneeded flashing scene for her too.
Unnamed guy working for the Hubbards	Machete to the stomach	Killed while he was peeping at Tina and Eddie having sex

6-13

Character	Means of Death	Notes
Tina	Stabbed in the eyes with a pair of hedge trimming shears	Her pre-kill sex scene with Eddie, at over 3 minutes long, was considered to be borderline porn. Editor Bruce Green was told to trim it up and make it look like a Pepsi commercial.
Eddie	Head crushed against a tree with a leather strap	
Anita	Throat slit	Anita's kill is unseen. Their singing duo while Demon is in the outhouse is one of the weirdest things ever.
Demon	Impaled with large metal spike while in an outhouse	
Junior Hubbard	Decapitated with a cleaver as he rode his motorcycle	Possibly the least effort put into a kill. All Roy had to do was hold out his arm with the cleaver and let Junior ride his motorcycle into it.
Ethel Hubbard	Cleaver thrown through window	Her head then falls into her stew.
Jake	Cleaver to the head	

Character	Means of Death	Notes
Robin	Machete pushed up through the bed	
Violet	Machete to stomach	
Paramedic Neil	Unknown	Unseen kill
Matthew	Spike through head and into tree	Unseen kill
Gramps/George	Unknown	Unseen kill
Killer – Tommy Jarvis (1)		
Roy	Pushed from hayloft, lands on a bed of spikes	
Killer – Dream Sequence Jason (2)		
Gravedigger 1	Machete to stomach	
Gravedigger 2	Some sort of spike to neck	
Killer – Dream Sequence Tommy (1)		
Pam	Machete to stomach	

KILL INDEX

Jason Lives: Friday the 13th Part VI (1986)

Character	Means of Death	Notes
Killer – Jason (18)		
Hawes	Fist through chest and out the back with heart in hand	
Darren	Fence post into crotch, then flung over Jason's head	The first guy to shoot a gun at Jason.
Lizabeth	Fence post into her head	Was nearly hit with the fence post in her scene. She was supposed to jump to the side. Jason actor CJ Graham followed her movement when he wasn't supposed to. Actress Nancy McLoughlin was the director's wife.
Burt	Arm torn off as he is flung into a tree and impaled on a branch	In the spot where Burt's face hit on the tree, someone had carved a perfectly-sized smiley face. The cut-out was bloodied by Burt's face.

Character	Means of Death	Notes
Larry	Triple decapitation with one swing of the machete	The deleted portion of this scene panned down to show their heads on the ground as their bodies had a synchronized fall.
Stan		
Katie		
Roy	Unknown	Unseen kill. You can see Dan Bradley as Jason in the scene where Roy shoots him with a paintball gun. The size difference between him and CJ Graham, who took over as Jason for the rest of the film, is clear.
Martin	Broken whiskey bottle to the throat	
Steven	Machete	Stabbed through both their chests at once
Annette		
Nikki	Head smashed into bathroom mirror and wall in the RV, leaving a face indentation	Actress Darcy DeMoss was previously seen in Axel's Aerobicise-watching scene in *The Final Chapter.*

Character	Means of Death	Notes
Cort	Hunting knife through the side of the head	
Sissy	Head twisted off	Some may recognize actress Renee Jones from her longtime role as Lexie Carver on *Days of Our Lives.*
Paula	Slashed	Unseen; some sort of blood spatter was shown. She was then thrown through window and pulled back in
Officer Thornton	Small metal spike thrown into forehead while on the dock	
Officer Pappas	Skull crushed with bare hands	If Darren didn't manage to hit Jason at close range earlier in the film, then Officer Pappas claims the distinction of being the first to actually shoot Jason.
Sheriff Garris	Grabbed by the neck and bent backwards in half	

KILL INDEX

Friday the 13th Part VII: The New Blood (1988)

Character	Means of Death	Notes
Killer – Tina Shepard (1)		
Mr. Shepard	Used her telekinetic powers as a young girl to destroy the dock and drown him	
Killer – Jason (15)		
Jane	Metal tent spike through the throat and into tree	
Michael	Spike thrown into his back	He crawled away. Jason lifted him by the spike and pulled it out as he threw him
Dan	Hand through the chest from behind then snapped neck	Dan supplied Jason with a machete for this film.
Judy	Smashed into a tree while in her sleeping bag	
Russell	Axe handle to the head	
Sandra	Drowned	Heidi Kozak had three stuntwomen the drowning scene: two for underwater shots and one that was dragged ashore.

6-13

Character	Means of Death	Notes
Maddie	Sickle to stomach	Unseen kill
Ben	Head crushed from top to bottom	All the other heads have been crushed side to side.
Kate	Noisemaker party horn into her eye	
David	Butcher knife into stomach	
Eddie	Machete to side of the neck	
Robin	Thrown out a second story window	Originally a machete kill, but the shots didn't look very good. The film crew had all returned to L.A. before it was noticed, so they changed it to her being thrown out a window to her death. She was thrown from the window of the house formerly used as the Jarvis's house in *The Final Chapter*.
Amanda Shepard	Long-handled grass hook into her back and through stomach	

Character	Means of Death	Notes
Dr. Crews	Cut in half with a weed whacker that had a saw blade attachment	
Melissa	Axe to head	

KILL INDEX

Friday the 13th Part VIII: Jason Takes Manhattan (1989)

Character	Means of Death	Notes
Killer – Jason (16 plus 3 unconfirmed)		
Jim	Harpoon to stomach	
Suzi	Harpoon driven into her chest	
J.J. Jarrett	Smashed in head with a guitar	
Unnamed boxer	Hot stone driven into his stomach while in the sauna	
Tamara	Stabbed with a piece of a mirror	
Jim Carlson	Stabbed repeatedly in the back with a spear of some sort	
Admiral Peterson	Throat slit from behind with machete	
Eva	Strangled with bare hands	Jason's first actual strangling with his hands. Actress Kelly Hu's first feature film role.
Wayne	Electrocuted and caught on fire	The fire led to the hull breech.
Miles	Thrown off a mast while trying to climb and escape; impaled	
Deck Hand of Doom	Axe in back	Unseen kill

Character	Means of Death	Notes
Gangbanger #1	Drug needle in the back of the neck	
Gangbanger #2	Head smashed into a pipe	Unconfirmed kill #1 of the movie
Julius	Head punched off with a single punch	It rolled down, eventually landing in a dumpster.
Irish cop	Choked out as he is dragged into an alleyway	Unconfirmed kill #2 of the movie
Uncle Charles McCulloch	Drowned when his body is held upside down in a 55-gallon drum filled with nasty water	
Cook in diner	Thrown into mirror in the diner	Unconfirmed kill #3 of the movie
Sanitation worker	Wrench to the head	
Killer – Wayne (1)		
Unnamed ship worker	Shotgun blast (accidental)	Wayne lost his glasses
Killer – Rennie (1)		
Colleen Van Deusen	Car explosion	Rennie hallucinates while driving a cop car and crashes into a wall. The car explodes before she can get out.
Killer – Hull Breech (4)		
Four nameless students	Drowned	Gathered in the restaurant, which flooded when the hull was breached.

KILL INDEX

Jason Goes to Hell: the Final Friday (1993)

Character	Means of Death	Notes
Killer – Coroner Phil/Jason (11 / 1 unconfirmed)		
Assistant Coroner	Metal probe to the back of the head	
Morgue Guard 1	Unknown	Unseen kill
Morgue Guard 2	Unknown	Unseen kill. Kane Hodder played the guard and Freddy Krueger's arm, in addition to his role as Jason.
Five kills between Youngstown and Crystal Lake	Unknown	Unseen; confirmed by Robert Campbell on *American Case File.*
Alexis	Face slashed, unseen weapon	This is the only unknown weapon.
Debbie	Fence post through tent and her chest	Was having sex with Luke at the time
Luke	Unknown	Unseen, unconfirmed kill during sex with Debbie
Edna	Head crushed in car door	
Killer – Deputy Josh/Jason (1)		
Diana (Voorhees) Kimble	Knife sharpener thrown into her back	

Character	Means of Death	Notes
Killer – Robert Campbell/Jason (8)		
Officer Ryan	Head smashed into locker	
Officer Mark Officer Brian	Heads smashed together	Radio DJs who begged on-air to be in the film and got their wish.
Ward	Arm broken; thrown into front door of the diner	
Unidentified male diner customer	Head smashed through counter	Some claim a second customer got shot; what they see may be Joey B jump back as Shelby shoots at Robert Campbell.
Joey B.	Elbow to the face	Was trying to save Shelby
Shelby	Head dunked in deep fryer then thrown onto the grill	
Vicki	Pulled onto a rod of some sort that she had just put through Robert Campbell/Jason's stomach.	Many say this is a BBQ skewer. However, if you watch when she picks it up, it is standing with broom handles and mop handles. Why would a BBQ skewer be there?

Character	Means of Death	Notes
Killer – Jason (1)		
Creighton Duke	Duke handcuffed himself to Jason, Jason bear hugged the life out of him	The only Jason kill after he was reborn through his sister Diana
Coroner Phil	They all shriveled and died after Jason possessed their bodies and then left for a new host	
Deputy Josh		
Robert Campbell		
Killer – Jessica (1)		
Sheriff Landis	Magic dagger to stomach	Jessica thought he was possessed by Jason.
Killer – Steven (1)		
Deputy Randy	Slit throat with machete while he was possessed by Jason	

KILL INDEX

Jason X (2001)

Character	Means of Death	Notes
	Killer – Jason (21)	
Soldier Johnson	Unknown	Unseen kill; had put a blanket over Jason's head
Soldier #2	Hits him in back of head with a rifle.	
Soldier #3	Grabs by throat, then throws him at another soldier firing at him.	
Soldier #4	Hits him in the face with the pole of the neck tether.	
Soldier #5	Chain around neck, then yanked on it hard.	
Dr. Wimmer	Spear through back	
Sgt. Marcus	Thrown through door	Unseen kill
Adrienne	Face pushed into liquid nitrogen then smashed into the counter	Jason's first kill in space
Stoney	Machete to stomach	
Azrael	Broken back	These are their actual kills; hologram kills don't count!
Dallas	Slams head into wall, crushes skull	
Sven	Neck snapped	

Character	Means of Death	Notes
Condor	Impaled	Fell onto a drill bit after he was pushed over a railing
Geko	Machete	Throat slit
Kicker	Machete	Split in half
Briggs	Swinging on a big hook	Unseen kill
Luke	Machete slash	
Professor Lowe	Machete (presumed)	Unseen kill, but Jason has his decapitated head stuck on the edge of his machete
Crutch	Head smashed into an electrical board	
Janessa	Sucked out a hole in the ship	Jason made the hole with a punch
Holograms Killed by Jason (4)		
Azrael	Sliced in half	
Dallas	Decapitated	
Two nameless naked female campers	Bludgeoned	Both in sleeping bags. One camper is beaten with the other. The other is then hit against a tree.

Character	Means of Death	Notes
Self-kills (3)		
Kinsa	Crashes shuttle into the ship	Distraught over Stoney's death; locked self into the shuttle and tried to take off.
Waylander	Explosion	Detonates explosives the group had placed on the walkway while he was still in the walkway with Jason
Brodski	Sacrificed himself to grab Jason and they both get sucked into the atmosphere of the planet	

KILL INDEX

Freddy vs. Jason (2003)

Character	Means of Death	Notes
Killer – Jason (18)		
Trey	Machete to back multiple times	Was laying on a bed. After the stabbing, he was bent backwards as Jason bent the bed in half end to end.
Blake's Dad	Decapitated	Unseen kill. Happened while Blake was sitting next to him dreaming. He woke up and his dad's head fell off.
Blake	Machete slash	Unseen other than blood splatter. Slash was in the upper chest/throat area.
Frissell	Double impaling with metal spike off of some farm equipment	Was launched off the spike a very far distance.
Gibb		Was passed out and being attacked by Frissell when it happened.

Character	Means of Death	Notes
Teammate	Head spun till it was on backwards	He was actually listed as "Teammate" in the credits; not the most anonymous kill of the movie
Shack	Flaming machete through the back	Football player, stoner, drunk
Unidentified male	Flaming machete slash to chest	These six anonymous kills were random partygoers.
Unidentified male	Flaming machete slash to throat	
Unidentified male	Machete stab to chest	
Unidentified male	Machete slash to stomach	
Unidentified male	Machete slash to chest	
Unidentified female	Machete slash, unclear where as it is mostly unseen	
Westin Hills Security Guard	Crushed under a door	Unseen kill
Deputy Scott Stubbs	Electrocution	As Jason is being electrocuted himself, Stubbs tries going by him, but Jason grabs him and he gets electrocuted, then has his head smashed for good measure.

Character	Means of Death	Notes
Bill Freeburg	Sliced in half at the waist with machete	Freeburg was possessed by Freddy at the time and managed to give Jason a tranquilizer before being sliced up.
Charlie Linderman	Thrown backward into a wall, impaled on a shelf brace; bleeds out soon after	
Kia Waterson	Slashed in throat with machete, tossed into tree at same time	
Killer – Freddy Krueger (1)		
Mark Davis	Face slashed; burnt message into his back	Freddy's only non-flashback kill in the movie
Killer – Jason in Dream Sequences (3)		
Heather	Machete to stomach and into tree	Freddy induced this dream sequence to wake Jason up. It was Jason's dream, therefore I believe it shouldn't count in the overall kill total.
Unnamed male	Heather morphs into these two.	
Unnamed female		

KILL INDEX

Friday the 13th (2009)

Character	Means of Death	Notes
Killer – Unnamed Female Counselor (1)		
Mrs. Pamela Voorhees	Decapitated with machete	Much like the original kill, but this time we see Jason comes up right after.
Killer – Jason (13)		
Wade	Machete slash to head and neck	His ear was chopped off with a headphone still in it.
Amanda	Stuffed in sleeping bag and strung up above the fire	Essentially roasted alive
Mike	Machete (presumed)	Unseen kill; stabbed multiple times, then pulled through the floor
Richie	Machete to top of head	Machete is driven half way down his head.
Donnie	Machete slash to the throat	Removed Jason's potato sack before being killed. As Jason picked it up, he spotted a hockey mask and opted for it instead.

Character	Means of Death	Notes
Nolan	Arrow through head	Jason uses a bow and arrow for the first time; hits his target perfectly as target was moving in a speed boat.
Chelsea	Machete through top of her head	Hides under the dock after being hit in the head with the boat and spotting Jason. Jason stabs the machete through the dock and into the top of her head. It lifts her out of water then she falls back in.
Chewie	Screwdriver into throat and up into skull	Chewie grabbed the screwdriver and tried to stab Jason, but he turned it around on him.
Lawrence	Axe through back and out chest	Jason throws the axe into his back. Lawrence still alive and screaming. Jason stands him up, turns him around and pushes him backwards. Axe is shoved out his chest, and he finally dies.

Character	Means of Death	Notes
Sheriff Bracke	Fire poker through eye and into front door of Trent's house	Jason dropped down behind him from the roof.
Bree	Mounted on a set of antlers	She is hung back first on antlers that were on the back of the bathroom door.
Trent	Stabbed in chest with machete then impaled on back of a tow truck as it drives away	The old man driving was Mr. Garikes
Jenna	Machete in back and out chest	As Clay was trying to pull her from Jason's lair.

ANSWERS

AM I EVIL?

1) June 13th, 1946. The year is calculated because he drowned in 1957 at the age of eleven.
2) Pamela Voorhees. Her maiden name is unknown.
3) Elias Voorhees. He was not officially named in the films until *Jason Goes to Hell: The Final Friday*. He was supposed to appear at the end of *Jason Lives: Friday the 13th Part VI.*
4) Diana Kimble. She is most likely his half-sister by a different mother. Mrs. Voorhees states that Jason was an only child. By Diana's assumed birthdate, Elias had already deserted Pamela and Jason. This was also not revealed until *Jason Goes to Hell.*
5) Eternal Peace Cemetery, Forest Green. The name can be seen during *Jason Lives: Friday the 13th Part VI* as Tommy is being led out of town and takes a detour to show the Sheriff that Jason's body is gone.
6) 1957
7) 2008. Rowan points this out in *Jason X*.
8) Hydrocephalus. It is a condition where there is an abnormal accumulation of cerebrospinal fluid in the ventricles of the brain.

KILLER MOMMY

1) a. 1930
2) b. 1979. Dates for both birth and death can be seen on her headstone in *Friday the 13th: The Final Chapter.*
3) c. 5
4) b. Cook
5) a. Sweater. Ginny Field tries wearing the sweater in Part 2 to fool Jason.
6) c. 1980. This goes against the entire timeline of the original films, which clearly started off with her being killed in 1979. However, there actually was a June 13th, 1980 on the real calendar.

CAMP CRYSTAL LAKE

1) 1935. This can be seen on the sign at the camp.
2) The Christy family
3) Camp Blood
4) New Jersey
5) Steve Christy
6) Wessex County
7) Forest Green. The name was changed back shortly after the events of *Jason Lives: Friday the 13th Part VI.*
8) Cunningham County
9) Camp No-Be-Bo-Sco. It is a Boy Scouts of America summer camp located in Blairstown in northwestern New Jersey. No-Be-Bo-Sco, which stands for "North Bergen Boy Scouts," is a functioning camp which has been operated continuously since the summer of 1927. As such, tourists and fans must call to make arrangements before visiting the site.

6-13

#SLASHTAGS

1) c. *Friday the 13th Part 3*
2) f. *Jason Lives: Friday the 13th Part VI*
3) k. *Freddy vs. Jason*
4) g. *Friday the 13th Part VII: The New Blood*
5) a. *Friday the 13th (1980)*
6) j. *Jason X*
7) l. *Friday the 13th (2009)*
8) d. *Friday the 13th : The Final Chapter*
9) b. *Friday the 13th Part 2*
10) e. *Friday the 13th : A New Beginning*
11) i. *Jason Goes to Hell: The Final Friday*
12) h. *Friday the 13th Part VIII: Jason Takes Manhattan*

CAMP COUNSELORS

1) Annie. Actress Robbi Morgan likened her character to Janet Leigh's character Marion Crane of *Psycho*, who gets killed off early in the film.
2) Alice Hardy. The scene where the snake is killed is a real snake being killed. The idea came from Tom Savini, who found a snake in his cabin.
3) Mike. The wheelchair led to one of the most memorable kill scenes in all of the films where his chair rolled back off the porch and down a flight of steps.
4) Motorcycle accident
5) Paul Holt
6) Sandra Dyer
7) Darren and Lizabeth
8) Sissy

6-13

THE MEN BEHIND THE MASK

1) True. Costume designer Ellen Lutter was used to portray Jason's legs at the start of *Friday the 13th Part 2.*

2) Ken Kirzinger. Kirzinger stood in as Jason for Kane Hodder in a few scenes of *Friday the 13th Part VIII: Jason Takes Manhattan.*

3) Richard Brooker

4) Kane Hodder. Hodder writes of the event in his autobiography, *Unmasked: The True Life Story of the World's Most Prolific, Cinematic Killer.*

5) Steve Dash. Dash did all of Jason's scenes with the exception of his legs in the beginning and when the unmasked Jason jumps through the window in the end. Actress Amy Steel mistimed one swing with the machete and it actually hit Dash in the hand. He had to be taken to the emergency room.

6) *The Final Chapter.* There were four actors shown as Jason: Ari Lehman, Steve Dash, Richard Brooker, and Ted White.

7) Ted White. He later said that he regretted the decision, as well as passing up the opportunity to portray Jason in the next film.

8) Ken Kirzinger. They wanted to give *Freddy vs. Jason* a David-and-Goliath feel. Kane Hodder, who had portrayed Jason for the previous four films, was 6 foot-2 inches tall, while Robert Englund was 5 foot-10 inches tall.

JASONS' RESUMES

1) Tom Morga
2) C.J. Graham. Although Graham did most of his own stunts, he went uncredited for them.
3) Ted White. He was 57 when he put on the mask for *The Final Chapter.*
4) Richard Brooker. He had been a restaurant patron on the show shortly before his death on April 8, 2013. They added the in memoriam tag after his episode aired a couple of weeks later.
5) Kane Hodder. Ed Gein also has another *Friday the 13th* connection. See page 50.
6) Derek Mears. He has also appeared in a number of episodes of FOX's *Sleepy Hollow.*
7) Ken Kirzinger. He was the diner worker that was thrown into a large mirror, and one of the three unconfirmed kills in the film.

6-13

TOWNSFOLK

1) Enos
2) Crazy Ralph
3) The Black Widows
4) Mr. Garikes
5) Ethel Hubbard
6) Martin
7) Playing paintball

GRIM FACTS

1) c. Elston Oil Supply. It can be seen on the side of the truck as he gives Annie a ride to The Crossroads.
2) a. The pantry. It is also where Alice found him hiding in the first film.
3) d. Harold and Edna
4) a. Abel
5) b. Ali, Fox, and Loco
6) b. Axel
7) a. Lana
8) d. Pete and Vinnie

6-13

IT FEELS LIKE THE FIRST TIME

1) *Jason Lives: Friday the 13th Part VI*
2) *Friday the 13th Part 3.* Parts 4, 7, 9, and the 2009 reboot were also released on Friday the 13th.
3) *Friday the 13th Part VIII: Jason Takes Manhattan.* Eva was portrayed by actress Kelly Hu. It was her first appearance in a feature film.
4) *Halloween: Resurrection*
5) *Jason Lives: Friday the 13th Part VI.* It was by Darren or Officer Pappas. Darren might not have hit the mark when he fired.
6) An axe. It was at the end of *Friday the 13th Part 3.* Chris Higgins hit him in the head with it, creating the familiar notch seen in the mask in Part 4.
7) Mark Davis

I SLASHED THE SHERIFF

1) c. Officer Dorf
2) f. Deputy Winslow. He had stumbled upon Jason's shack in the woods and saw his shrine to his mother.
3) b. Deputy Scott Stubbs. He was the only member of law enforcement to think Jason was involved, and the only one to try and help.
4) d. Sheriff Michael Garris
5) a. Sheriff Ed Landis
6) e. Officer Randy Parker

THIS TIME (WILL BE THE LAST TIME)

1) 1979. It was June 13, 1979. Mrs. Voorhees says it was Jason's birthday. Then, in *The Final Chapter*, her headstone clearly says she died in 1979.
2) 1984. Paul Holt points out it has been five years since Mrs. Voorhees's murderous rampage.
3) 2455

Which came first?

A. Jason was shot for the first time. It happened in Part VI. His first strangling was Part VIII.

C. Richard Brooker portrayed Jason Voorhees. He was in Part 3, while Ted White was in *The Final Chapter.*

F. Jason Voorhees electrocutes someone to death. It was Chuck in Part 2. Jason isn't struck by lightning until the beginning of *Jason Lives.*

G. Paul Holt runs a site near Crystal Lake. Paul Holt ran Packanack in Part 2, and Matthew Letter ran Pinehurst in *A New Beginning.*

I. A dog named Gordon appeared in the movies. Gordon was Tommy Jarvis's dog in *The Final Chapter.* Toby was Rennie Wickham's dog in *Jason Takes Manhattan.*

L. We were introduced to Higgins Haven. It was in Part 3, while we didn't see the Eternal Peace Cemetery until *Jason Lives.*

WHAT A PAIR

1) b. Chuck and Chili
2) d. Tina and Terri. Camilla More auditioned for the role of Samantha. When producers found out that she had a twin sister (Carey More), the roles of Tina and Terri were offered.
3) f. Jeff and Sandra. Their kill scene had to be cut short to avoid an X-Rating. Sandra's brother Rob would come looking for Jason in *The Final Chapter*.
4) e. Demon and Anita
5) c. Waylander and Brodski. Waylander blew up the pontoon of the ship that he was trapped in with Jason. Brodski launched himself at Uber-Jason before he had a chance to get back into the ship. The two would be sucked into the atmosphere of Earth II.
6) b. Trent and Jenna. Jenna was just trying to be nice to Clay and help him in his search for his sister. Trent was jealous of this and decided to sleep with Bree.
7) a. Andy and Debbie. Debbie mentions this in Chris's van as the police sirens approach them from behind and everyone begins eating the marijuana to get rid of it.

A WHOLE OTHER DIMENSION

1) b. Popcorn
2) d. Yo-yo
3) a. Harpoon gun. It was Jason's first kill while wearing the hockey mask. The harpoon's destination was Vera's left eye.
4) c. Rick

COOL KILLS

1) Chuck. He is shoved backwards into a fuse box.
2) An outhouse
3) Judy. In the scene, Kane Hodder smashed the sleeping bag with a dummy in it against the tree multiple times; it was cut to just once for effect.
4) Weed Whacker with saw blade attachment. The original scene apparently showed Dr. Crews cut in half, but it was one of the many cuts made to avoid an X-Rating.
5) Julius. His head then rolled through a few obstacles and landed in a dumpster. The lid then slammed closed.
6) Janessa
7) Condor
8) His own bladed hand. This was a perfectly ironic way to finish off Freddy Krueger.
9) Nikki. The final shot of her face leaving the imprint was filmed underwater with a piece of plastic.
10) Nolan
11) Corkscrew
12) Flare (lit)
13) Adrienne. This kill scene included a great camera shot from the bottom of the sink.
14) Charles McCulloch. He had previously been shown to push a 14-year-old Rennie out of their boat and into Crystal Lake, where she nearly drowned.
15) Mr. Garikes. You can see the tow truck parked outside of Garikes's barn earlier in the film.
16) Party horn noisemaker

6-13

THE MASKS OF DEATH

1) A potato sack. In a *Freddy vs. Jason* flashback dream scene, we see a group of kids tormenting a young Jason by putting a similar sack over his head.

2) Shelly. He emerges from the lake wearing the mask in an attempt to scare Vera, who was sitting on the dock. He then ventures off into the barn, where he meets up with Jason.

3) Detroit Red Wings. The mask was taken from a crewmember's bag. He was known to always have hockey equipment with him. Prior to that it was planned to use an umpire's mask instead. Good thing there was a hockey fan on-set!

4) Blue markings, rather than red

5) Eastern Hockey League. One of the funniest Jason moments in all of the films is as he turns and "looks" at the camera briefly after seeing the billboard with the image that looked just like him.

6) Jim. Jim had the mask on board to be used to scare his girlfriend Suzy after telling the story of Jason.

7) Tommy Jarvis tossed it onto his corpse. He had planned to burn it along with Jason.

8) *Friday the 13th Part VIII: Jason Takes Manhattan.* He does this in Times Square when the group of kids gives him a hard time about him just destroying their boom box.

9) Donnie. He had pulled off the sack that Jason had been wearing to that point. Jason saw the hockey mask as he reached for the sack.

DO IT AGAIN

1) b. Whitney. We saw Jason raise the machete to hit her with it, but then the title card comes on the screen and we do not know her fate until later when Clay and Jenna find her alive.
2) a. Outpost
3) c. Lucille. His super-bong had its own plush carrying case.
4) a. Beer Pong
5) a. Richie. He was running back to camp after hearing Amanda screaming as she was stuffed into her sleeping bag and hung above the fire.
6) c. Archery and hockey. After seeing Nolan's kill shot that Jason made with his bow and arrow and knowing Jason's affinity for the hockey masks, we can assume these trophies were his and well deserved.
7) c. Hockey stick
8) a. Wok and fire poker. We must remember he did just finish using Chewie's bong Lucille.
9) c. Wood chipper
10) c. Combos, Fritos, and Funyuns

6-13

SPACE ODDITY

1) Cunningham Realty
2) ANTS
3) *Grendel.* The name was taken from the novel *Beowulf.*
4) Earth II. Original Earth could no longer sustain life and was a vast wasteland.
5) Hockey. They had to explain what Jason was wearing on his face to part of the crew.
6) *Solaris.* Writer Todd Farmer joked in an interview how there were probably 20,000 people on the space station who could be added to the kill count.
7) Microsoft Conflict
8) Kinsa
9) Uber-Jason
10) Four: Azrael, Dallas, and two female campers. The first two were doing battle with dinosaur-like creatures when they were interrupted by Jason. The two campers were used as a diversion to buy some time for the remaining crewmembers to find a way to stop Uber-Jason.
11) d. 4420. As Adrienne is recording her findings, she mentions this specimen number.

CAMPFIRE SONGS

1) Pseudo Echo. The song is being played during Violet's kill scene.
2) "Down in the Valley" and "Michael, Row Your Boat Ashore"
3) "Tangerine" by Johnny Mercer
4) "Teenage Frankenstein" by Alice Cooper. His song, "He's Back (the Man Behind The Mask)," was made for the film and used as its theme.
5) WGAZ, The Electricity of Manhattan. This can be heard in the opening scenes with Jim and Suzy on their boat. The DJ sends out a dedication to the graduating class at Lakeview High.
6) "Sister Christian" by Night Ranger
7) AC/DC's "Back in Black". Glover has said in interviews that that was how he actually danced in clubs at the time, and that this was the song playing during his actual dancing.
8) David Bowie. These disguised titles led to many former cast members auditioning for the new film, only to then have to back out because they had been in a previous installment in the franchise.

THE FIRST JASON

1) Irwin Keyes. Ari talks about how he was the comedian on-set in his foreword in this book.
2) Jazz piano
3) "Machete Is My Friend." This is the author's favorite song by the band.
4) Sand Pond
5) Harry Manfredini
6) Westport, Connecticut. Ari originally auditioned for them at the Westport Y.M.C.A.
7) Four hours

POP GOES THE WORLD

1) c. *Fangoria.* It included an article about special effects genius Tom Savini and an article celebrating the 25th anniversary of *Godzilla.*

2) c. The Arsenio Hall Show. Arsenio pulled off the hilarious interview without Hodder saying a single word.

3) c. American Excess. The card can be seen floating in the mud puddle right after her kill scene.

4) b. KISS

5) d. Zaxxon

6) b. Bruce Springsteen. You can also see stickers for the following bands/artists inside her van: The Grateful Dead, The Doors, The Rolling Stones, Tom Petty, and Led Zeppelin. Also on her front bumper are stickers reading "I Love Skiing" and "Snow Bunny."

7) a. *A Place in the Sun*

8) b. "I'll be back!" The other choices were from *Top Gun*, *Back to the Future* (actually said by Glover), and *Fast Times at Ridgemont High.*

9) c. A pen used in high school by Stephen King

10) b. *Saturday the 14th*

11) a. Statue of Liberty

12) a. Mickey Mouse. She is wearing it during the orientation meeting in the beginning.

13) c. Sony Walkman

14) d. Pac-Man

15) d. *Star Wars*

TOMMY, CAN YOU HEAR ME?

1) 12
2) Unger Institute of Mental Health
3) *The Goonies*
4) Roy (the paramedic). He pushes him from the barn loft and he lands on a bed of spikes.
5) Allen Hawes. He was portrayed by Ron Palillo, better-known as Arnold Horshack on *Welcome Back, Kotter.* Jason thrust his fist into Hawes's chest, and it emerged out his back with his heart in his hand. I always felt that Paililo's death scene would have been better if he screamed "Eww, Ewww Ewww, Eww" like he did on the TV show.
6) Pam Roberts. At the end of *A New Beginning*, Pam may have been killed by Tommy, if it wasn't a dream sequence. The original plan, though, was to bring Pam and Reggie back for Part VI. This makes one think it was indeed meant to just be a dream.
7) Jason Bateman

VS. THE PAST

1) Westin Hills Psychiatric Hospital. It is also the setting for many parts of the *Nightmare on Elm Street* story.
2) Nancy Thompson. She just kept coming back for more in the original films. Now she lives on in this film, too.
3) KRGR. Glen was portrayed by Johnny Depp in the original *A Nightmare on Elm Street.*
4) Tina Gray
5) "How sweet, dark meat!"
6) Springwood Slasher. He was a prolific child kidnapper and pedophile who managed to become even worse once parents killed him by burning down the building he was staying in.

6-13

JASON NEVER FORGETS

1) d. *The Final Chapter.* Trish Jarvis hits him between his fingers with a machete, slicing him open.
2) b. Put a sack over his head. This helps explain why Jason chose to wear a potato sack in Part 2.
3) c. Deborah Voorhees. Despite being a kill by Roy, this is one of the most memorable cool kills of the franchise.
4) a. Jeff and Sandra

HE'S GOT ISSUES

1) b. Leatherface. The story explains how Jason escapes custody and hops on a train. He winds up with Leatherface and family. They welcome him in, but he always remains an outsider.
2) d. Doris
3) c. *Satan's Six*
4) a. Freddy and Ash. There was also a previous series that was just Freddy vs. Jason vs. Ash.

PROPPING IT FORWARD

1) e. *From Dusk Till Dawn* (1996). It was used as Monkey Man's heart. (See #6 below)

2) c. *The Evil Dead* (1981). Sam Raimi used it without permission from its creator, Tom Sullivan.

3) d. *Ed Gein* (2000). Kane Hodder would portray Gein in a different film.

4) a. *The Birds* (1963)

5) b. *Creepshow* (1982). It was used in the segment titled "The Crate." (See #7 below)

6) Tom Savini. The heart was ripped out by Fred Williamson's character, Frost, and was still beating in his hand. Savini took what looked like a large toothpick and used it as a stake to kill the heart.

7) Fluffy. The creature was a sort of demonic-looking baboon with lots of extra teeth and was created by Tom Savini for the film.

HODDER THAN HELL

1) Three. Once when he is blown up in the beginning, again as security guard #2, and finally as Jason in the end when Jessica drives the Magic Dagger into his heart.
2) Michael. He was killed in the woods and never made it to the party.
3) a. Standing in Times Square in full costume. He said he felt like a rock star when everyone stopped what they were doing, watched him, and cheered at times.
4) Dr. Crews
5) Admiral Robertson
6) Wayne Webber
7) Phil. Actor Richard Gant had a very hard time eating the prop heart which for that scene was made of gelatin and filled with fruit cocktail that was in a black dye.
8) *Unmasked*
9) Tamara
10) Creighton Duke
11) *Hatchet*
12) Azrael
13) Kay-Em 14
14) Luke
15) c. Swinging Judy in her sleeping bag against a tree. He now has a new favorite kill of all-time in his role as Victor Crowley in the *Hatchet* films.

6-13

I'M DRIVING IN MY CAR

1) e. Chris Higgins
2) a. Megan Garris
3) c. Ginny Field
4) b. Pam Roberts. Tommy Jarvis then drives it in Part VI.
5) d. Mrs. Pamela Voorhees. Steve Christie also drove one of these Jeeps.
6) Cobra
7) Cadillac Escalade
8) December
9) "The Serpent"

THE ONE THING

1) 6. A boat marked #29 can clearly be seen after the battle, as well as a third one on which the number cannot be seen clearly.
2) *Friday the 13th Part VII: The New Blood.* It is on the Shepards' car as they arrive at the lake.
3) 76 Union Gasoline. Can be seen out the windshield of the car before Ali smashes it in.
4) 8th. Can be seen on the overhead sign as they enter. It was, however, a fake entrance, as all interior subway scenes were filmed on sets.

Matching:

1) f. #81. He is wearing it in the scenes leading up to his kill scene.
2) g. #88
3) b. #10. Can be seen while the group prepares for breakfast.
4) e. #66
5) d. #37
6) c. #13. Can be seen as he leaves the infirmary after having his arm reattached.
7) a. #8. It is on the jacket he wears through most of the film.

ROUNDABOUT (IN AND AROUND THE LAKE)

1) c. Victor J. Faden
2) b. Jarvis Sandwich
3) a. Crazy Ralph. Walt Gorney delivered the narration.
4) b. *American Case File*
5) d. *Friday the 13th Part 3*
6) a. CG Cutter *Dallas*
7) b. Canada and Love
8) d. Freddy's Back
9) b. Colleen Van Deusen.
10) c. Whistles
11) a. Russell
12) a. Youngstown, OH
13) c. Beware of Bears
14) c. Joey B's. Shelby was her husband.
15) c. U.S. flag on a pole
16) a. Elizabeth Marcus
17) c. *Lady Drifter*
18) c. Reggie the Reckless
19) b. $500,000
20) a. Nintendo (NES)
21) b. Punch Out
22) b. Hellbaby
23) d. J.J. Jarrett. She was beaten to death with her own Flying V guitar.

DIRECTOR'S SLASH

1) *Manny's Orphans.* Actor Irwin Keyes, who portrayed the uncredited busboy in the original *Friday the 13th*, was also in this film.
2) *Halloween H20: 20 Years Later*
3) *Missing in Action* and *Invasion USA*. Both films starred Chuck Norris.
4) *The Last House on the Left*
5) Jason Voorhees's tombstone. McLoughlin has shared a story where a meter reader refused to enter his backyard to read the meter because he thought there was actually someone buried back there.
6) *Texas Chainsaw 3D*
7) *Bride of Chucky*
8) *Conan the Barbarian* and *The Texas Chainsaw Massacre*

STAGE FRIGHT

1) Catherine Parks. She was the fourth runner-up to Miss Ohio, Susan Perkins.
2) Jensen Daggett. She appeared in a 1984 episode of the game show.
3) Allison Smith
4) *The Last American Virgin*
5) Arnold Jackson (*Diff'rent Strokes*). Ross portrayed Dudley Ramsey on the show.
6) Kelly Hu. She was Miss Hawaii.
7) Jennifer Cooke
8) Arnold Horshack (Ron Palillo)
9) *Weird Science*
10) Leatherface, in the film *Leatherface: The Texas Chainsaw Massacre III*
11) *The Gingerbread Man*
12) *Andromeda.* In the show, their roles were reversed, with Ryder portraying a human and Doig the android.
13) Terry Kiser. The film was *Weekend At Bernie's.* Catherine Parks also appeared in this film.
14) Spartacus
15) *Joan of Arcadia*
16) Kelly Rowland
17) Peter Barton

JASON X-RATED

1) Danny Steinmann. *A New Beginning* was the final film he directed.
2) Deborah Voorhees
3) Nipples. They fall off shortly after he attaches them.
4) *Aerobicise*
5) Ted
6) *The Final Chapter.* The skinny-dipping scene put it over the top.
7) *Jason Lives: Friday the 13th Part VI.* There was one sex scene with Cort and Nikki, but no nudity anywhere.
8) Chewie
9) *Chic*
10) *Hustler*
11) Trent and Bree
12) Through her vagina. Actress Erin Gray was shocked when she saw the scene and was quick to point out she never posed in that position for that scene.
13) Tina
14) Marcie Cunningham. This occurred in her sex scene with Jack in the original *Friday the 13th*.
15) Michael Bay
16) Darcy DeMoss
17) Monopoly
18) America Olivio

BEHIND THE SCENES

1) c. Ethan
2) b. *Part VIII: Jason Takes Manhattan.* After the film did poorly at the box office, Paramount was happy to give up the franchise.
3) b. Josh. Victor Miller said that once the film began taking on a darker feel, he felt the name Josh didn't fit, so he stuck with the J name and came up with Jason.
4) d. *Halloween*
5) b. The bathroom
6) c. Tom Savini
7) a. *Carrie*
8) d. Los Angeles. There were going to be two rival gangs teaming up to take on Jason.
9) c. *Friday the 13th Part IX: The Dark Heart of Jason Voorhees*
10) a. Car. Palmer was paid $10,000 for 10 days of work.
11) b. Ki-ki-ki, Ma-ma-ma. He took "Kill her, Mommy" which was being said by Betsy Palmer and then said just the beginning sounds Ki and Ma into a machine called an Echoplex.
12) c.300 Gallons
13) d. Kevin Bacon
14) a. Wakeboarding
15) b. In his backyard. He was on a short break from filming *The Goonies.*
16) c. *Long Night at Camp Blood*
17) d. EverQuest

THIS IS THE END

1) *Jason X* and *Friday the 13th* (2009)
2) Mrs. Pamela Voorhees. This was a copy of the jump scene first used in the original, but in the end it didn't have the same effect.
3) Mr. Shepard. Tina uses her powers to call him for help. He rises up from the lake and drags Jason back down with him.
4) His machete and Freddy's head. Freddy winks and smiles at the camera, and then we hear his signature laugh as they walk off.
5) Toby the dog. Luckily, Kane Hodder refused to do a scene where he was supposed to kick the dog after emerging from the water in Manhattan. Hodder has explained how Jason would never hurt children or animals, at least in his mind.
6) Freddy Krueger's clawed hand. Kane Hodder is the person who reaches up and pulls the mask down.
7) A shooting star
8) His mask and the locket with a picture of his mother and himself

SOURCES

Sources included all of the following:

Movies and television:
Friday the 13th (1980)
Friday the 13th Part 2
Friday the 13th Part 3
Friday the 13th: The Final Chapter
Friday the 13th: A New Beginning
Jason Lives: Friday the 13th Part VI
Friday the 13th Part VII: The New Blood
Friday the 13th Part VIII: Jason Takes Manhattan
Jason Goes to Hell: The Final Friday
Jason X
Freddy vs. Jason
Friday the 13th (2009)
The Birds (1963)
Creepshow (1982)
From Dusk Till Dawn (1996)
A Nightmare on Elm Street
A Nightmare on Elm Street Part 3: Dream Warriors
A Nightmare on Elm Street Part 4: The Dream Master
His Name Was Jason: 30 Years of Friday the 13th (documentary)
The Arsenio Hall Show

Web:
IMDB.com
FirstJason.com
nobebosco.org
Fangoria.com
Screamhorrormag.com
fridaythe13thfilms.com
fridaythe13thfranchise.com
fridaythe13th.wikia.com
houseofhorrors.com

themovietimeline.com
campblood.net
maps.google.com
avatarpress.com
dccomics.com
WildStorm comics
comicvine.com
topps.com
azlyrics.com
nintendo.com
celestialseasonings.com
boxofficemojo.com
youtube.com
wikipedia.org

Books:
Unmasked: the True Story Of The World's Most Prolific, Cinematic Killer by Michael Aloisi and Kane Hodder

Individuals:
Ari Lehman
Alan Clague
James Maxwell
Richard Gray Pennington

LINKS

www.signaturehorror.com

www.samsonpublishingcompany.com

www.facebook.com/groups/613afridaythe13thmovietriviabook

www.facebook.com/fridaythe13thtriviabook

www.diogolando.com

Also available:

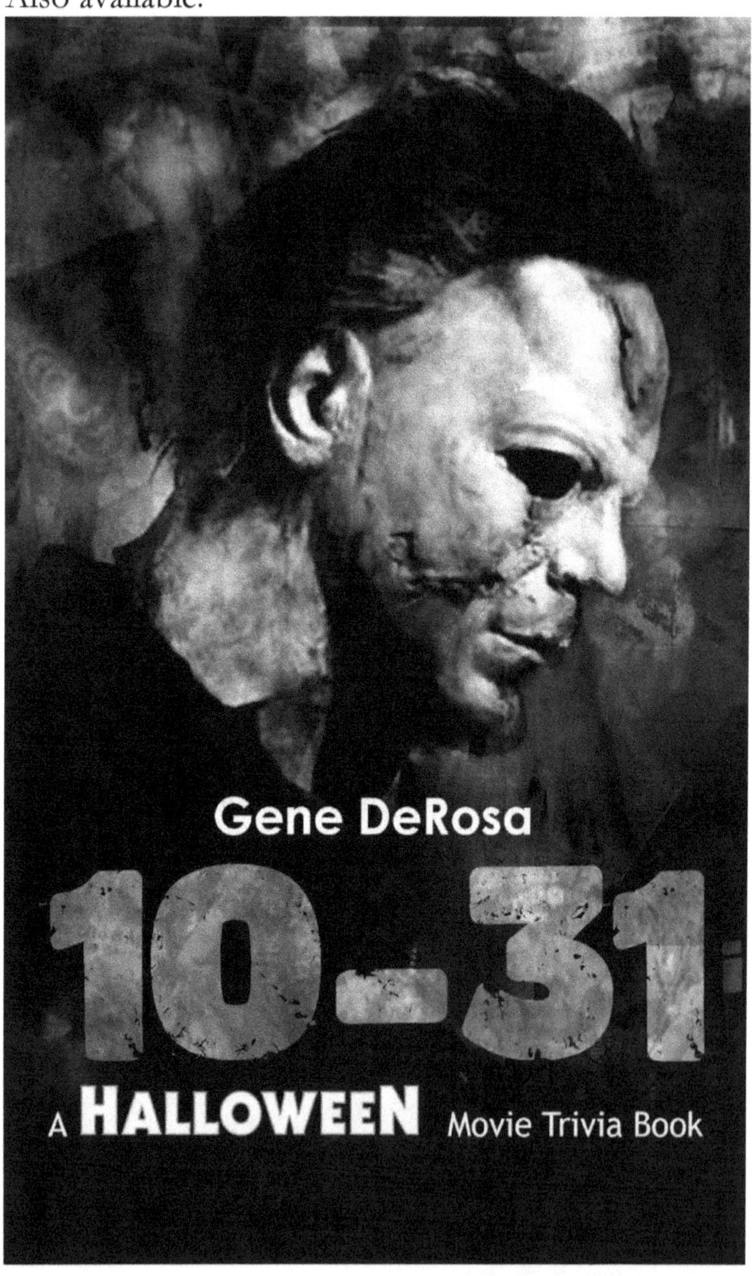

www.ingramcontent.com/pod-product-compliance
Lightning Source LLC
Chambersburg PA
CBHW070205060426
42445CB00033B/1537

* 9 7 8 0 6 9 2 2 4 2 3 4 6 *